ONE OF A KIND

PORTRAITS FROM THE LASALLE BANK PHOTOGRAPHY COLLECTION

ONE O

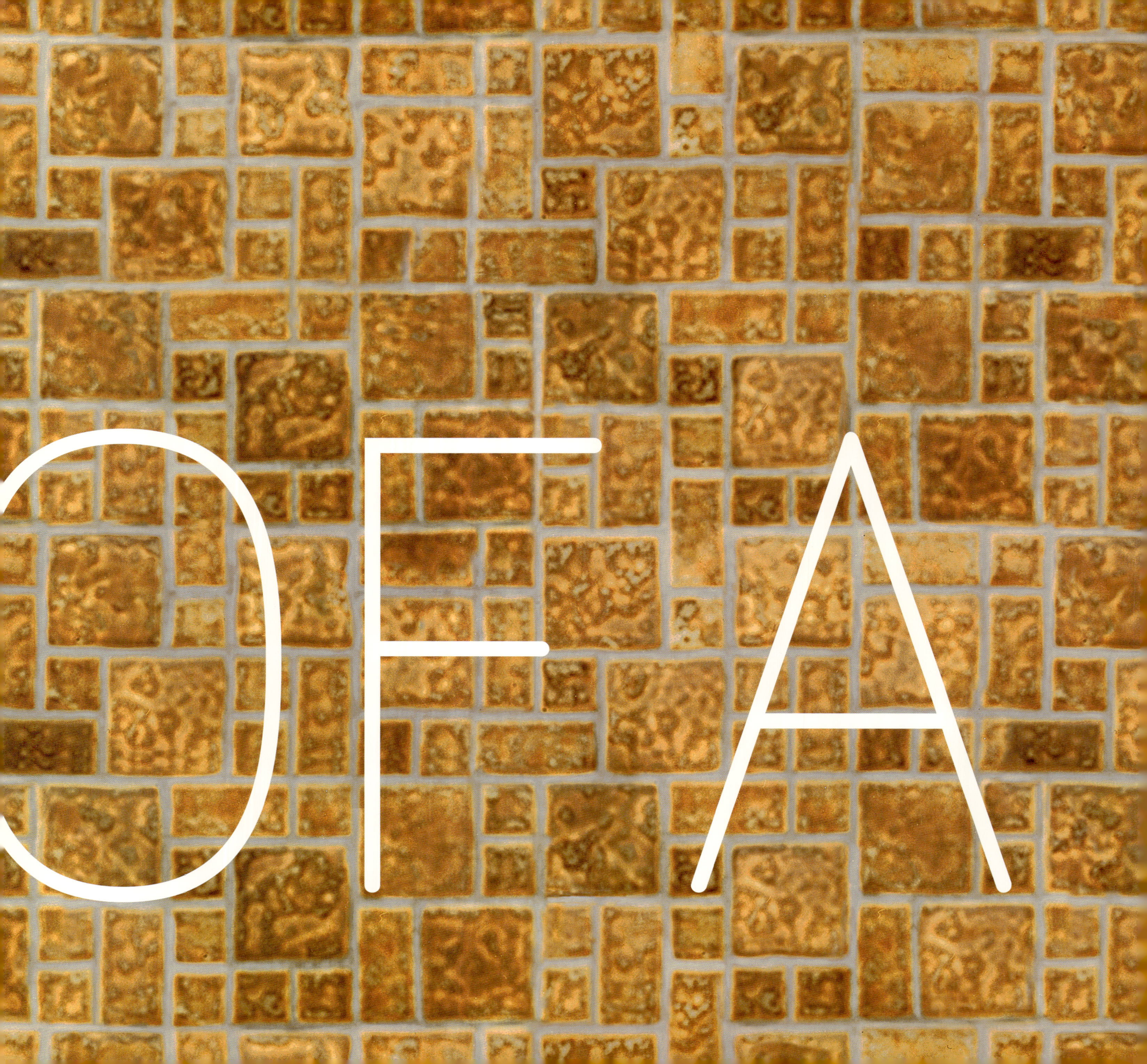
OFA

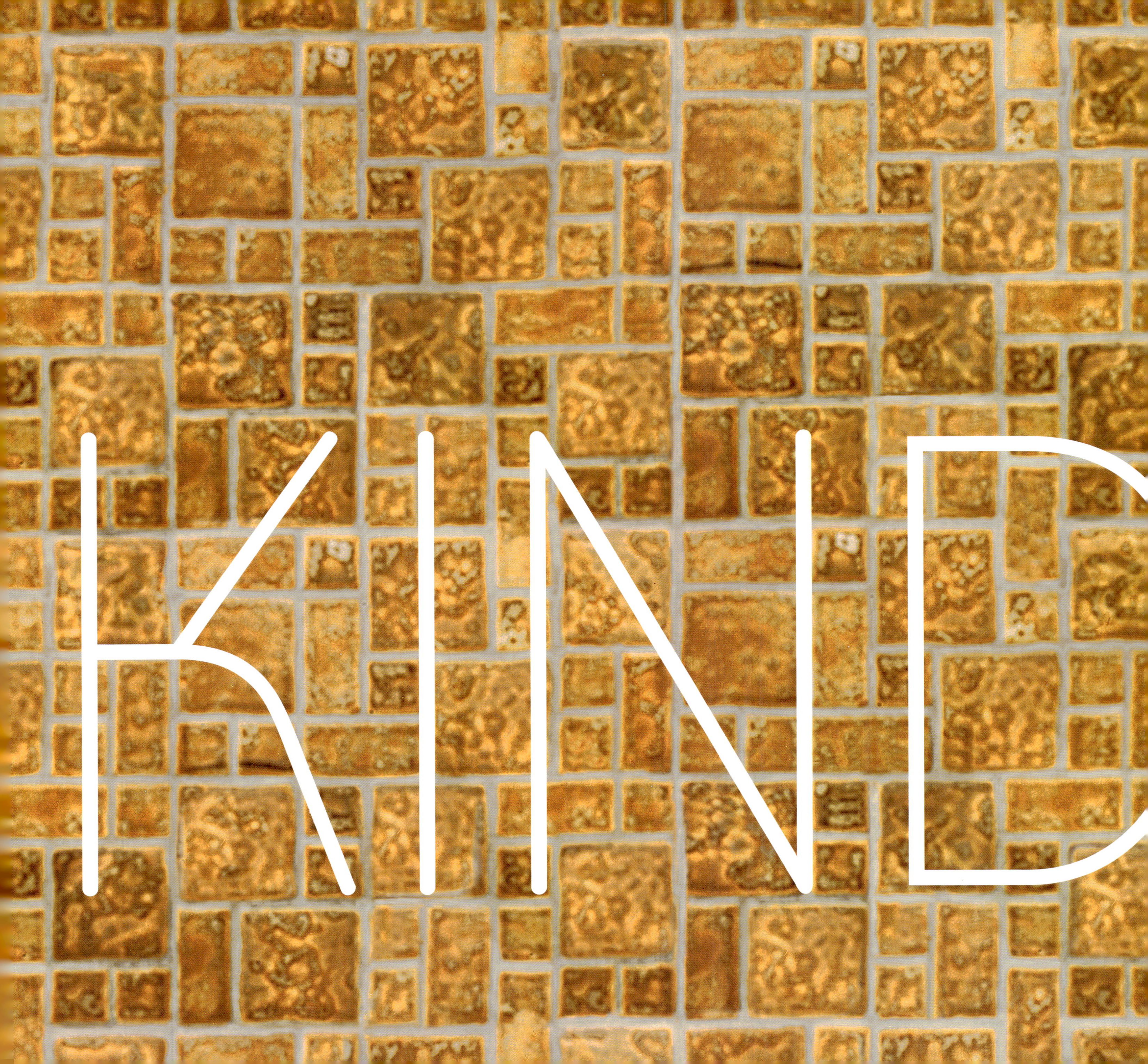
KIND

TABLE OF CONTENTS

FOREWORD

THOMAS C. HEAGY

ONE OF A KIND is the fourth book in a series of five on the LaSalle Bank Photography Collection. Its title is fitting for a book about portraits from our collection, for although the phrase implies uniqueness, inherent in the words is the connection to others – of being part of a group. As with the individuals portrayed, each photograph in this book stands alone as a work of art. When combined together, they illustrate the historical depth and artistic breadth of our renowned collection.

The LaSalle Bank Photography Collection is approaching its fortieth year. Ever since its inception, the mission of our collection has been to enrich the lives of all who come to the bank. To this end, the collection is on display throughout the halls, common areas, and offices of the bank. LaSalle's curatorial department has an ongoing educational program that includes publications on different aspects of the collection, rotating exhibitions, and employee lunch-time lectures featuring local and international photographers. I would like to thank Carol Ehlers, curator, and Whitney Bradshaw, assistant curator, who selected the images for *One of a Kind* from over 5,000 photographs in the collection, then sequenced them to enhance one another yet retain their artistic uniqueness.

The portraits in this book are a portrait of humankind – a focus of attention that mirrors our people-centered approach to banking. Just as the art in our collection enriches our workplace, it is through our employees and customers that LaSalle Bank comes to life.

THOMAS C. HEAGY
Vice Chairman, LaSalle Bank

PORT

RAITS

1 AUGUST SANDER *Savings Bank Cashier, Cologne* 1928

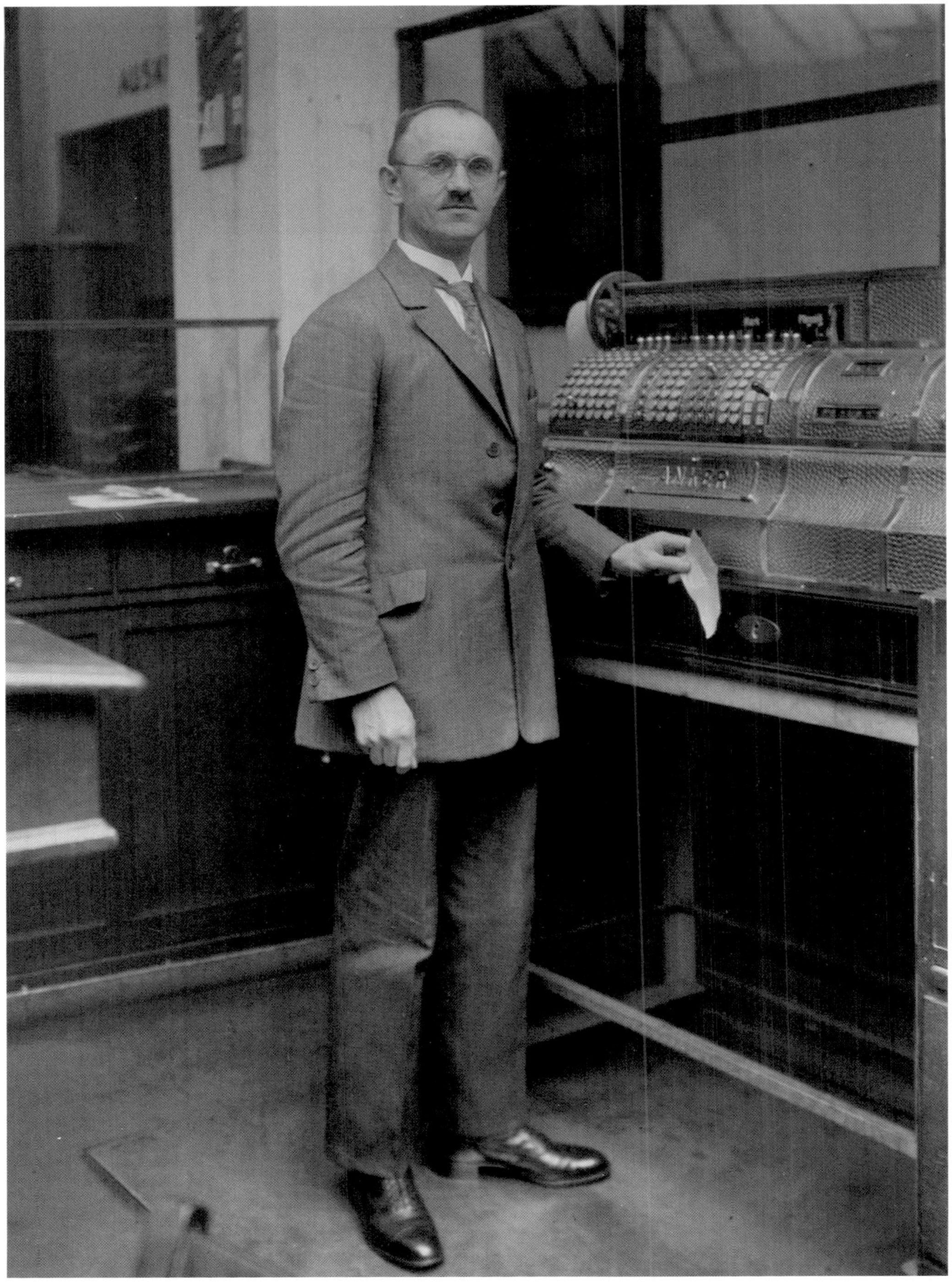

2 WALKER EVANS *Penny Picture Display, Savannah* 1936

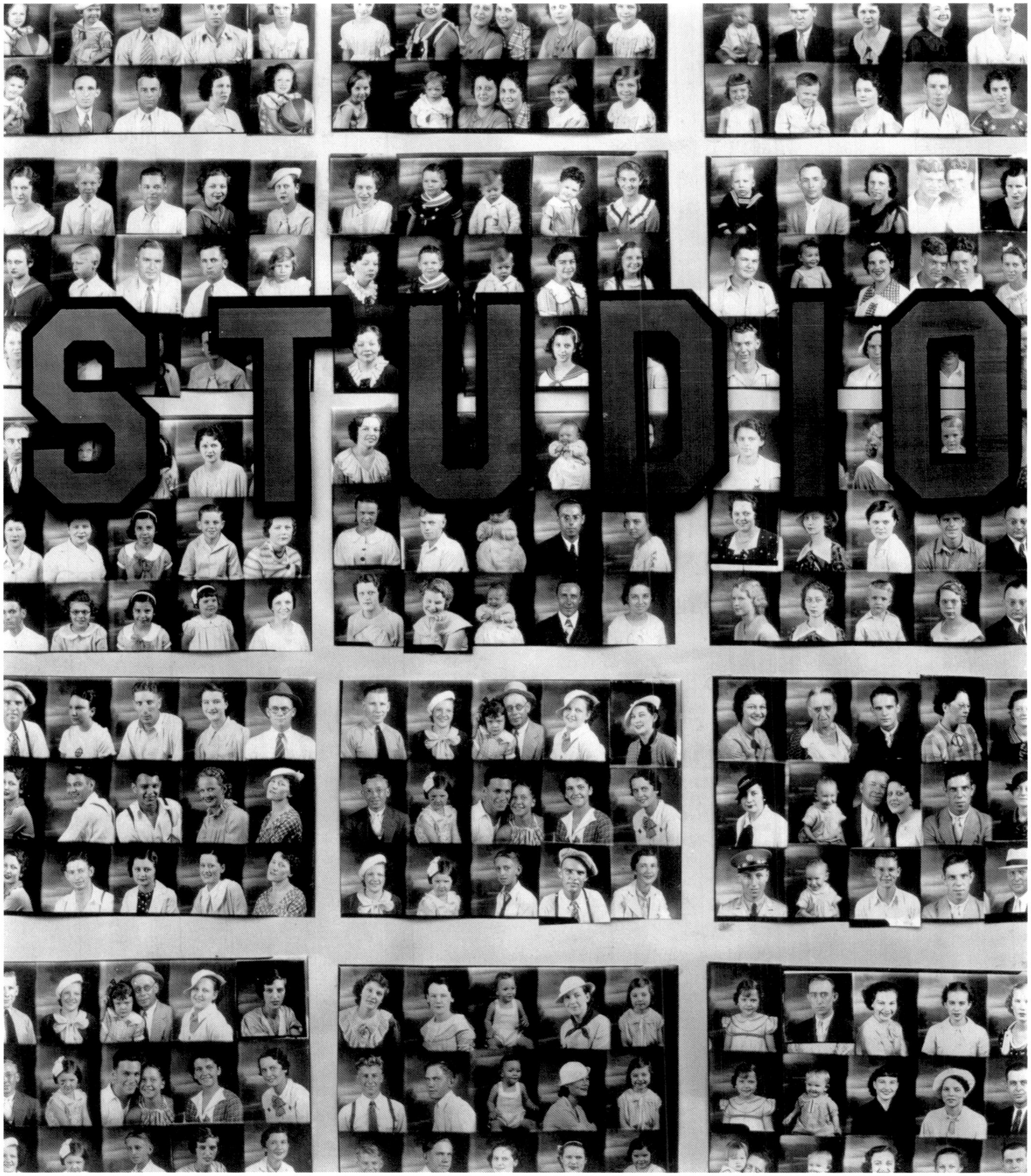
STUDIO

3 MIKE DISFARMER *Untitled (Heber Springs, Arkansas)* ca. 1940–45

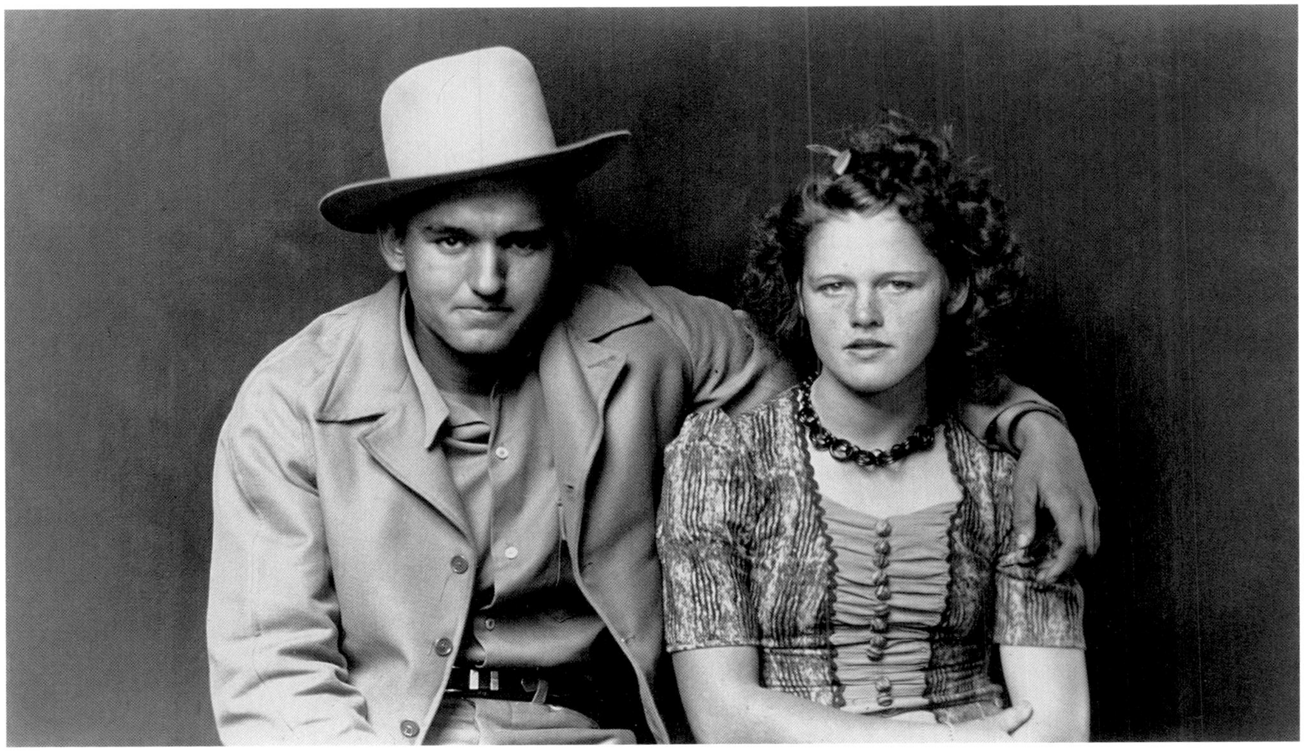

4 JULIE MOOS *Mrs. Carr and Mrs. Thornton* 2000

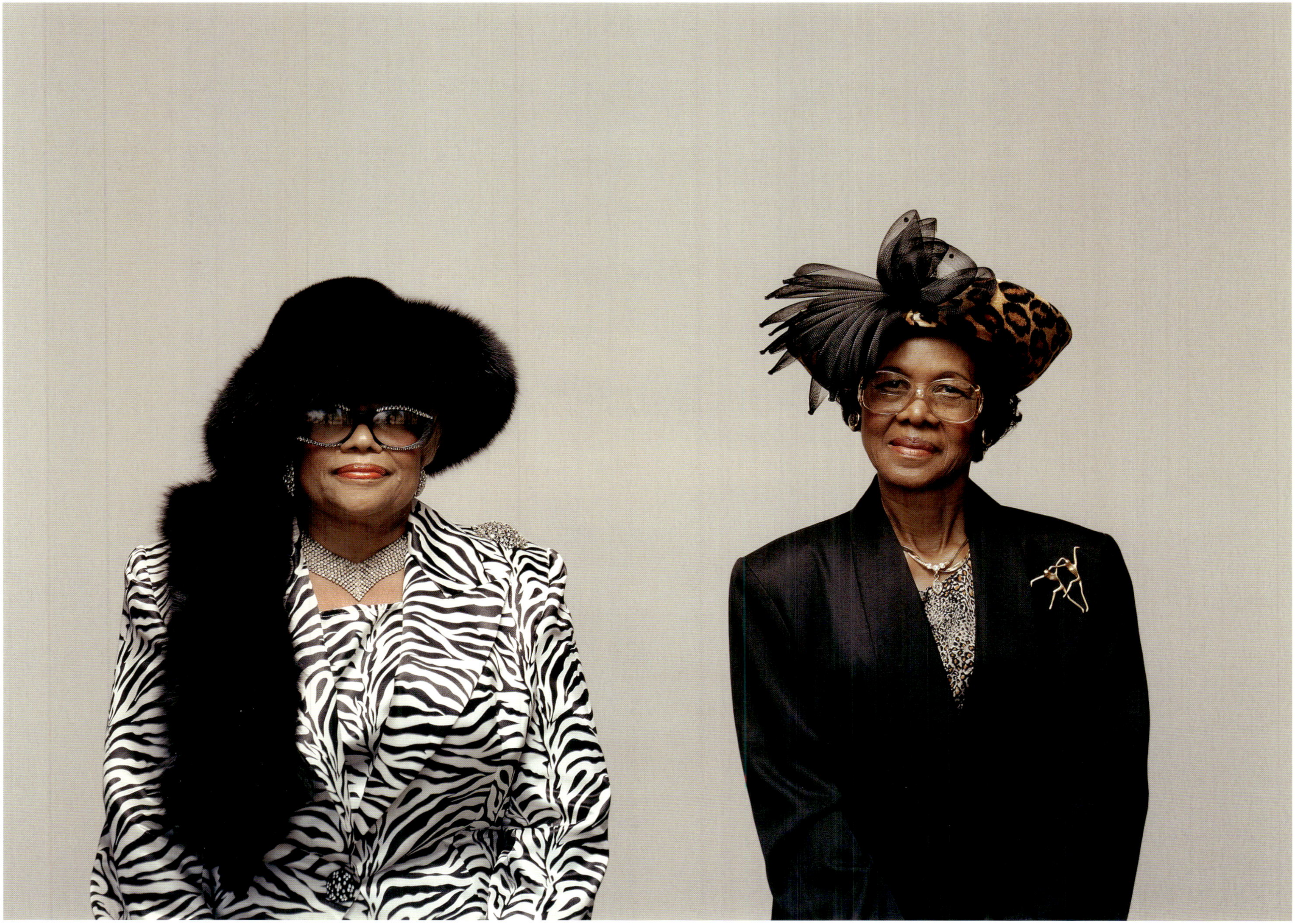

5 RICHARD AVEDON *The Duke and Duchess of Windsor, 1957* 1957

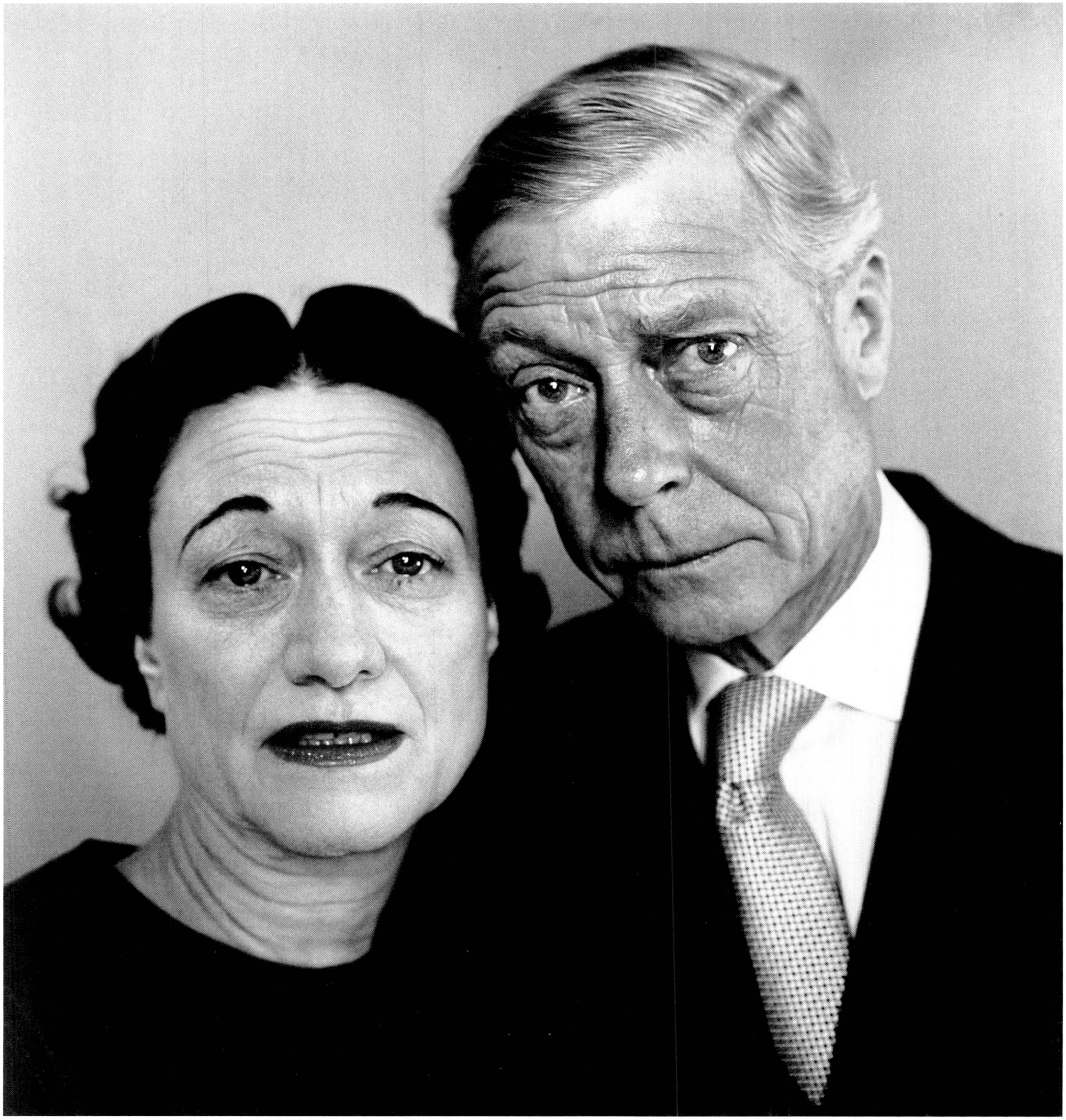

6 EDWARD WESTON *Tina Modotti, Mexico, 1924* 1924

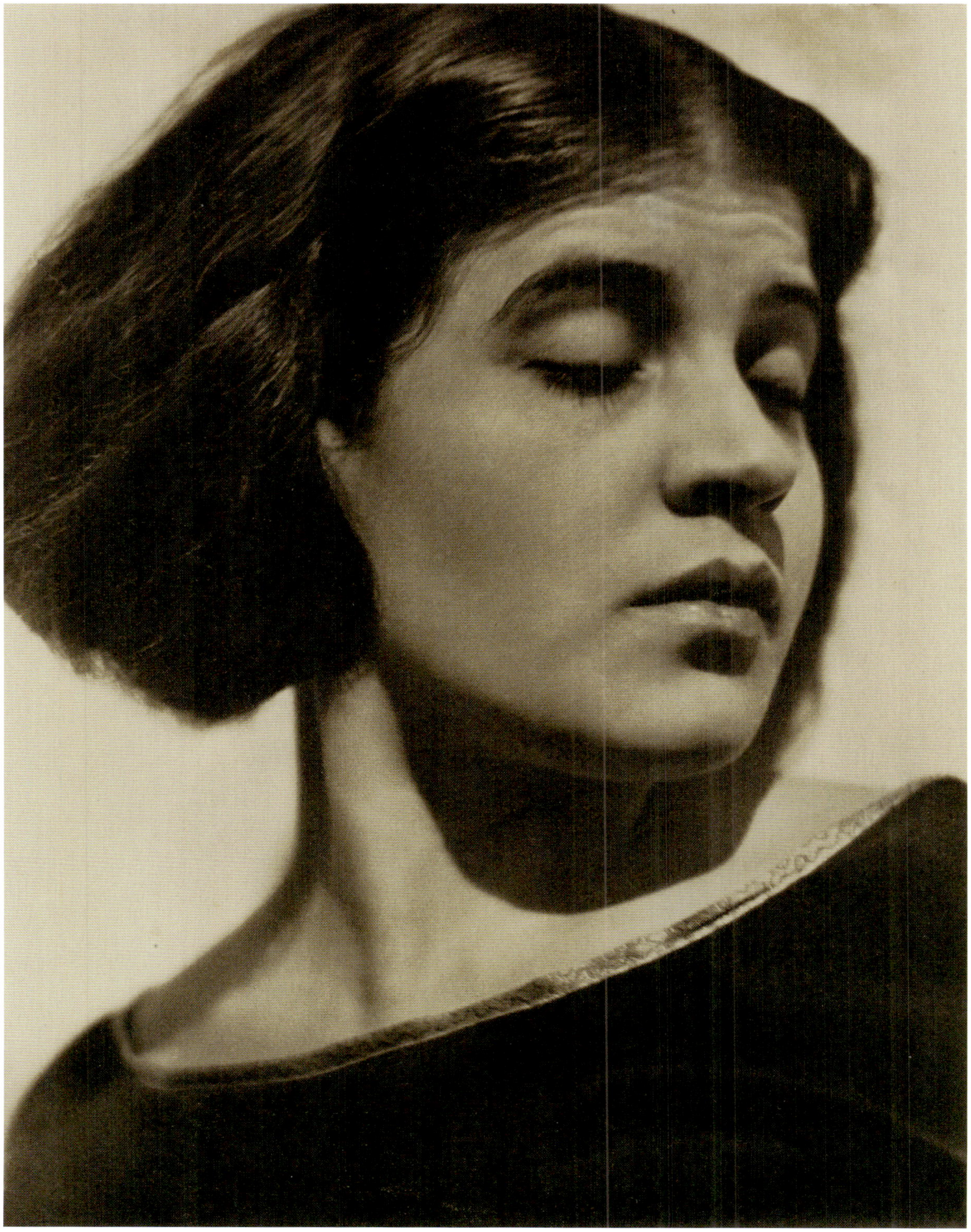

7 RICHARD AVEDON *Marilyn Monroe, Actress, 1957* 1957

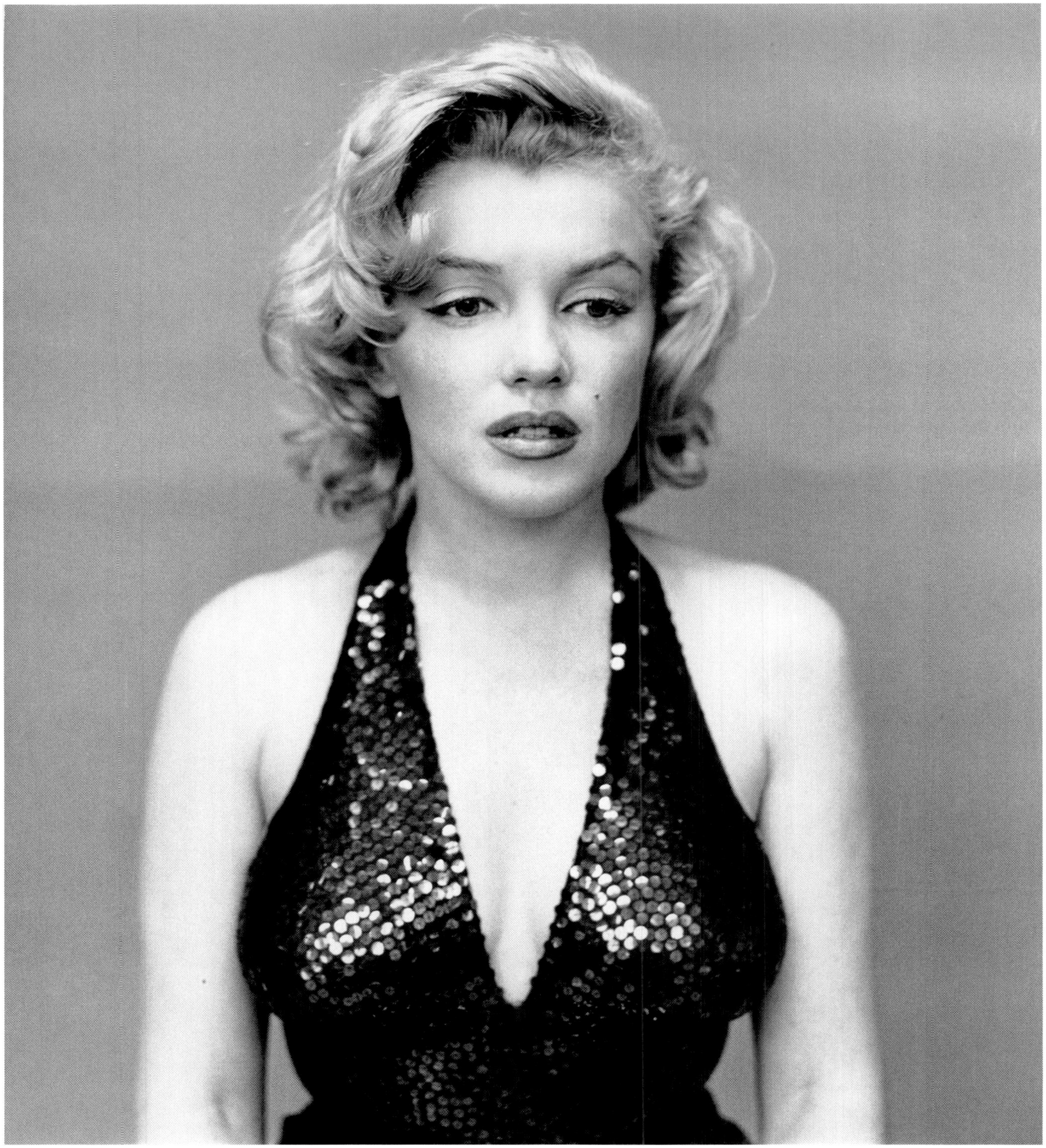

8 JULIA MARGARET CAMERON *Untitled (May Prinsep), October 1870* 1870

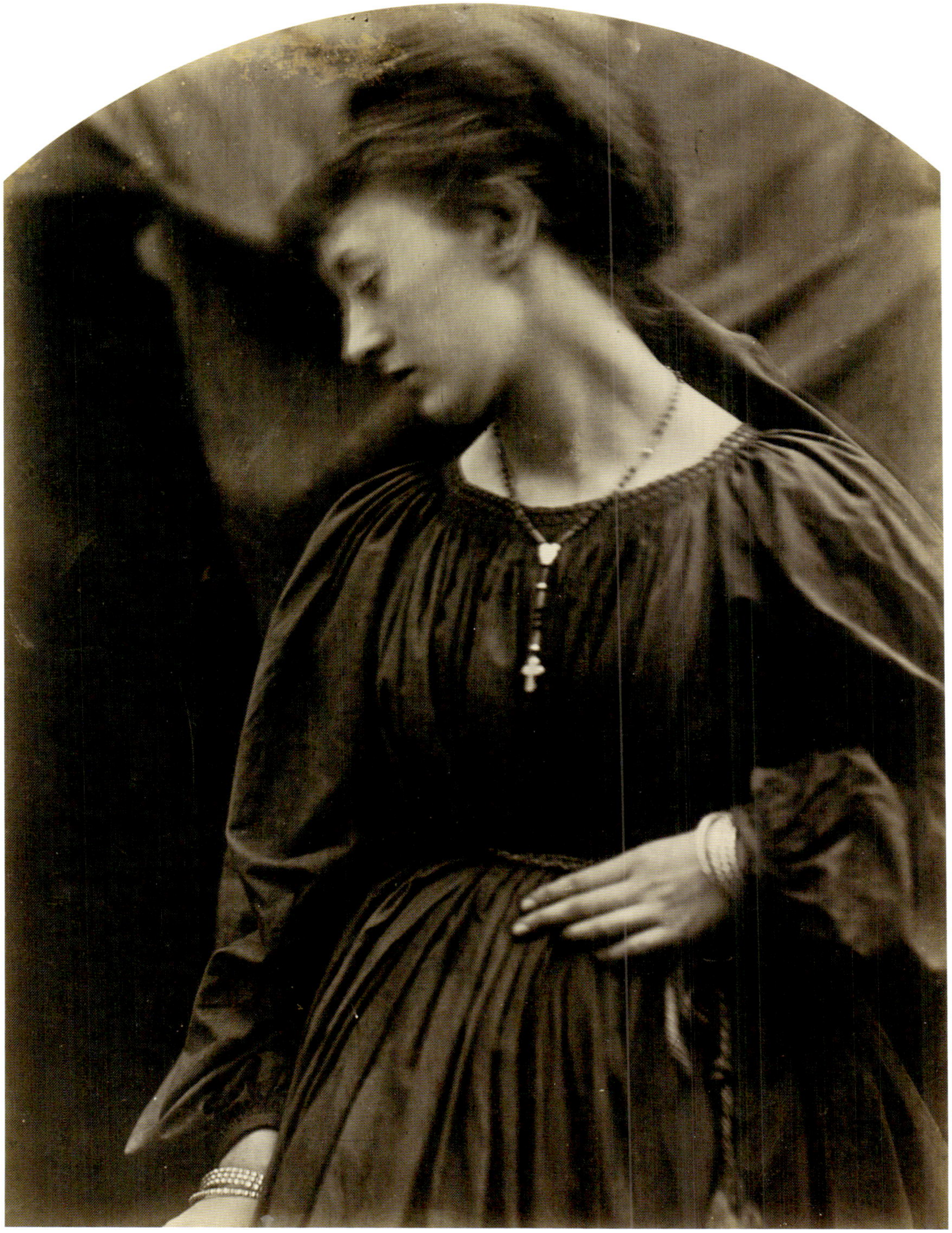

9 CINDY SHERMAN *Untitled Film Still #50* 1979

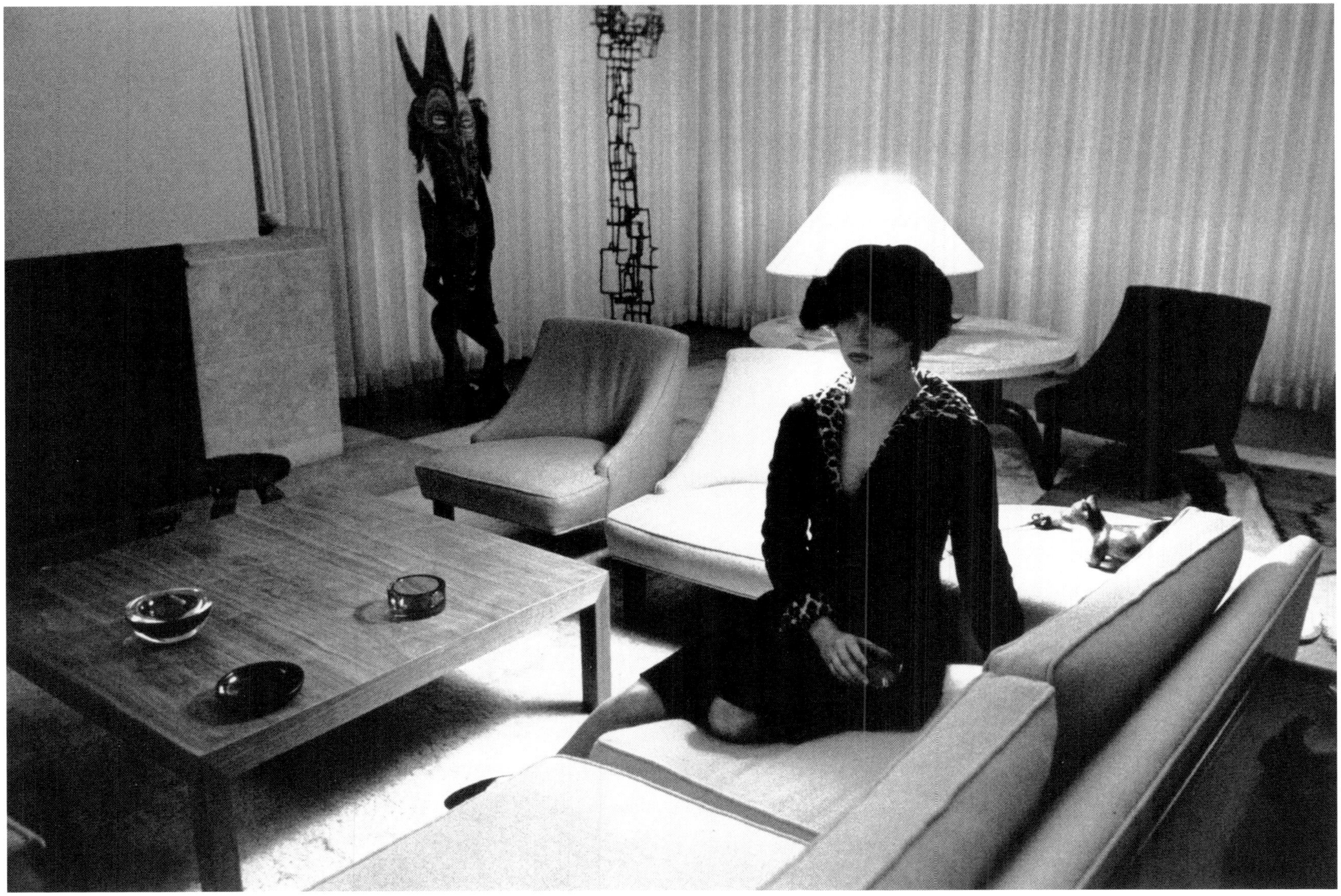

10 WILLIAM KLEIN *The Bride* 1955

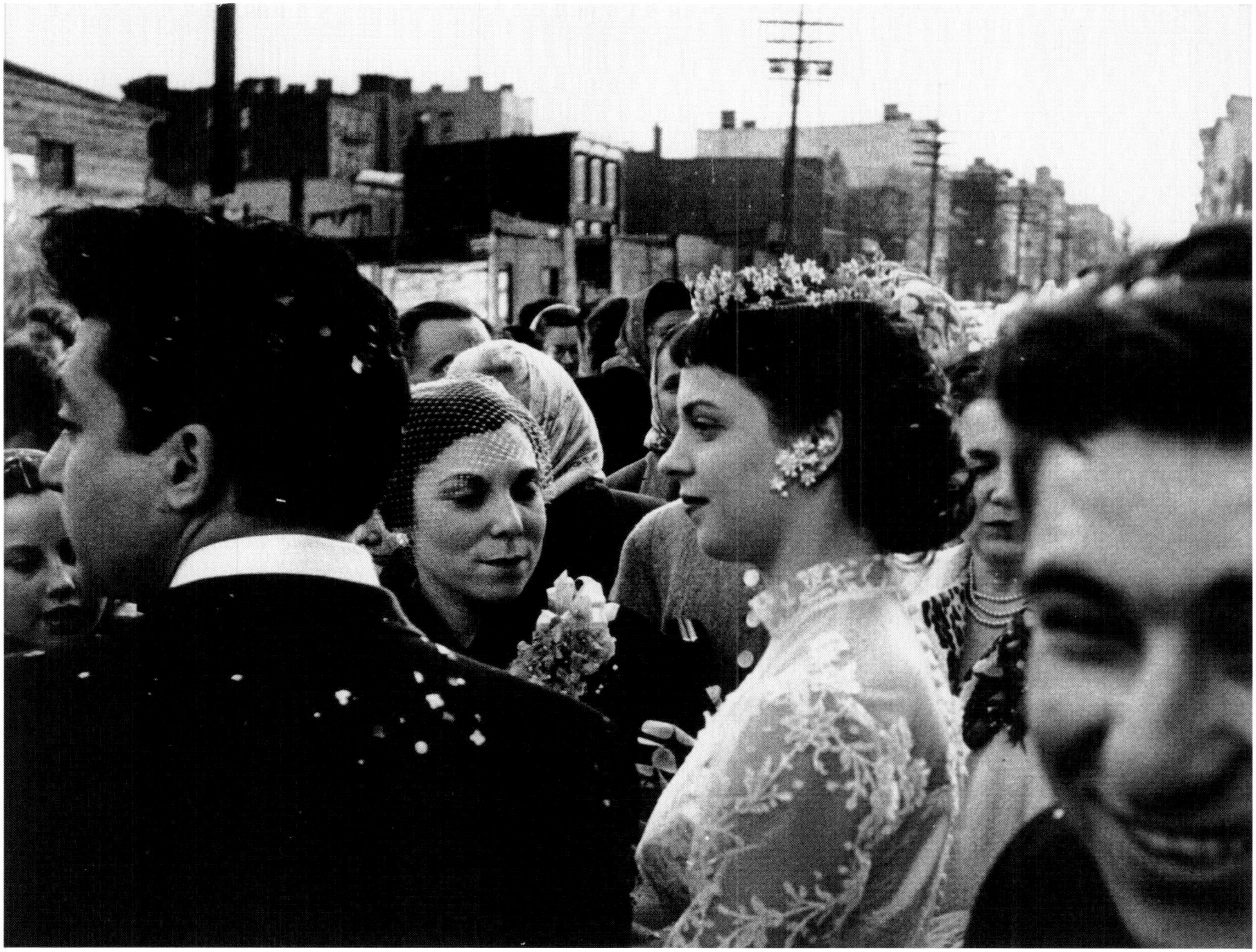

11 GORDON PARKS *Broke Price, former Hollis War Counselor, Harlem* 1948

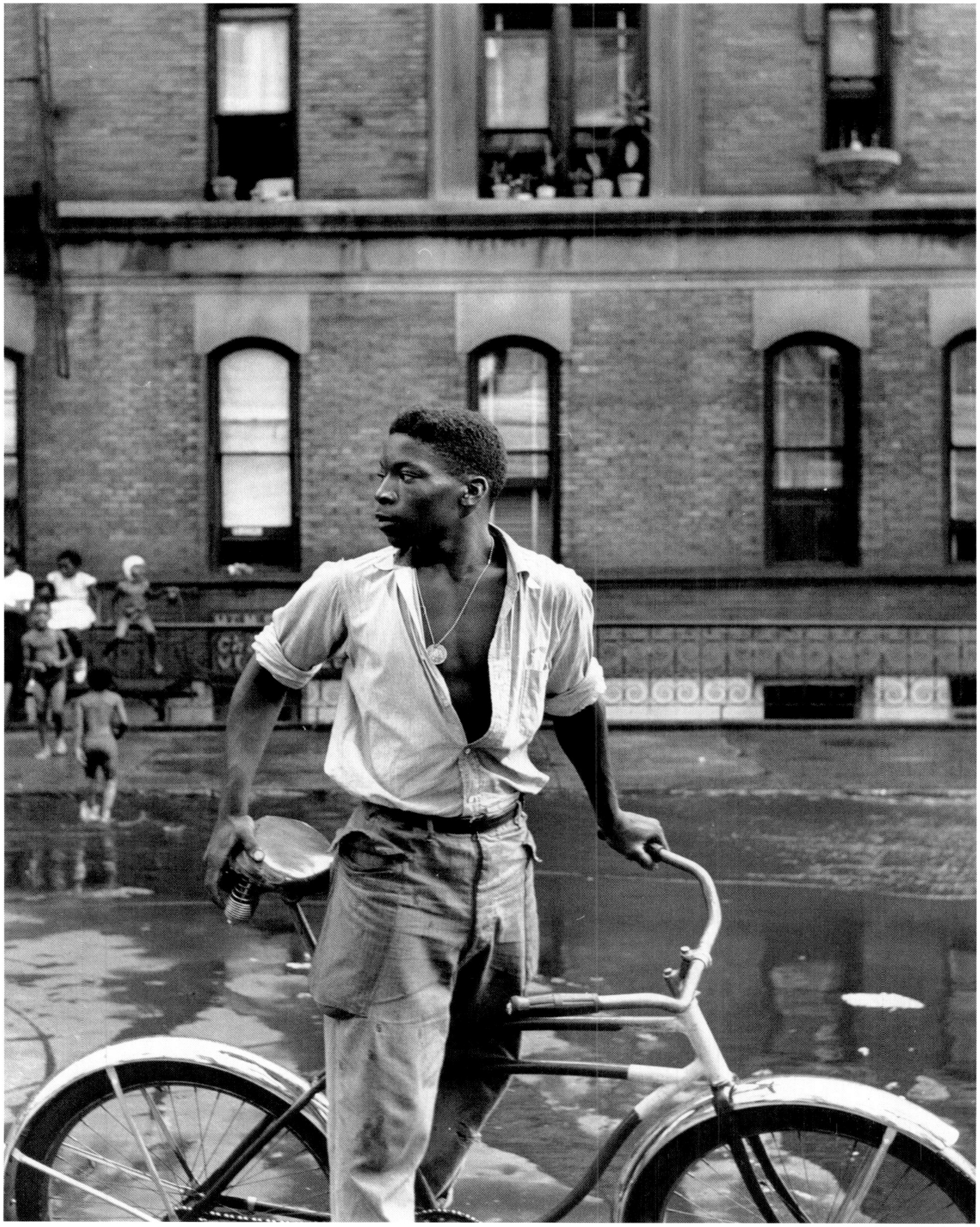

12 EDUARD VAN DER ELSKEN *Groenburgwal, Amsterdam* 1963

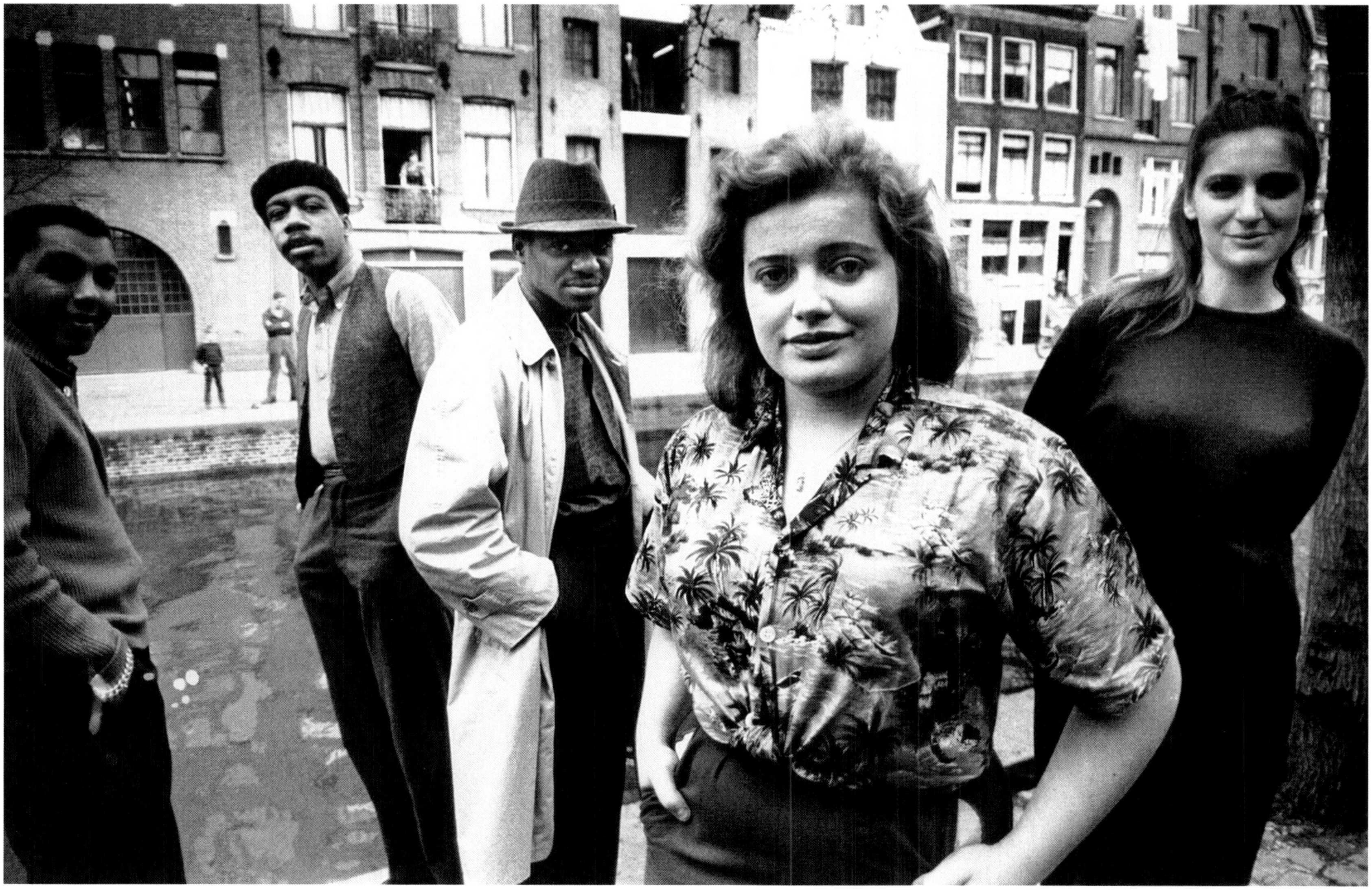

13 RINEKE DIJKSTRA *Vondelpark, June 10, 2005* 2005

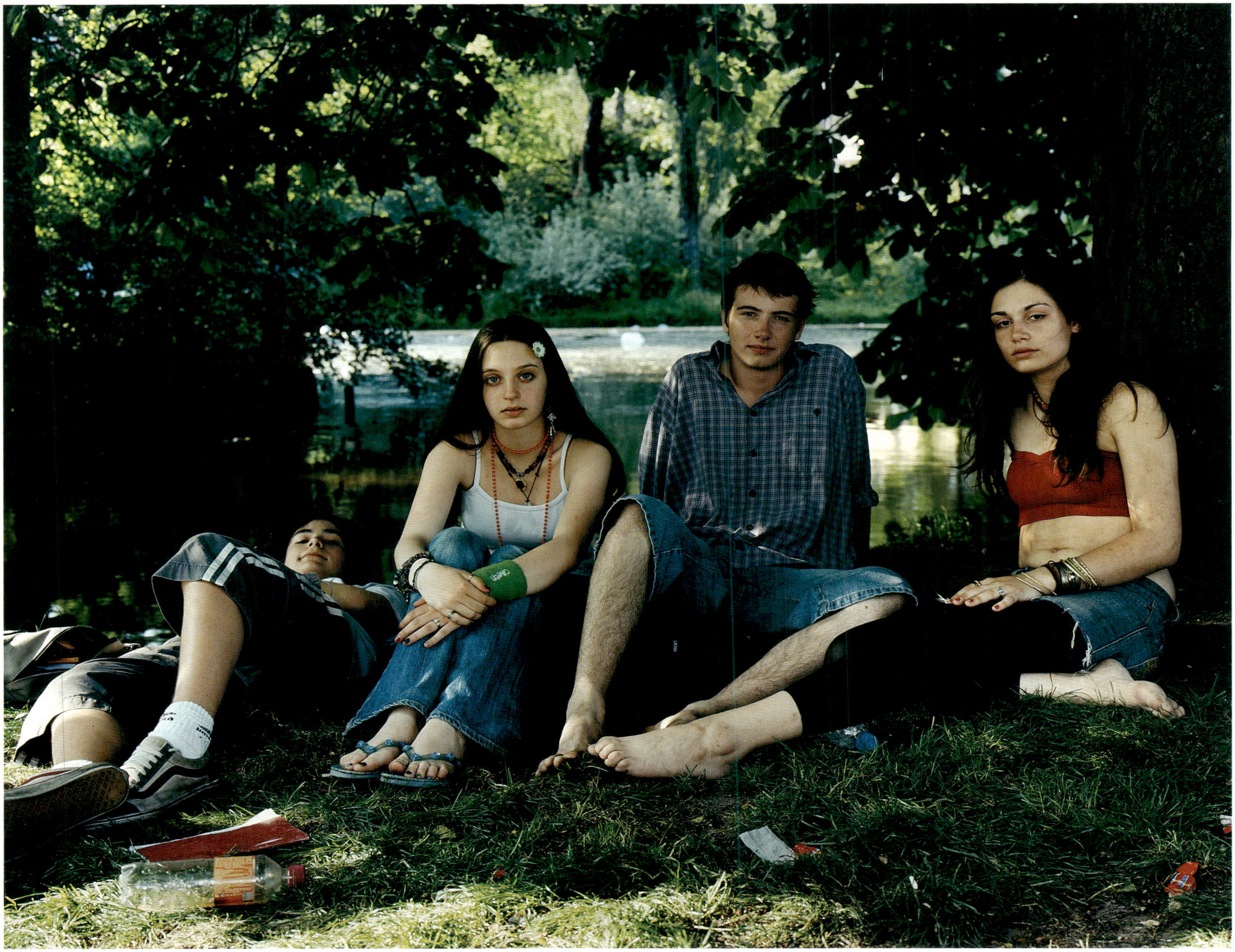

14 JITKA HANZLOVÁ *"Indian Woman," Chelsea* 1999

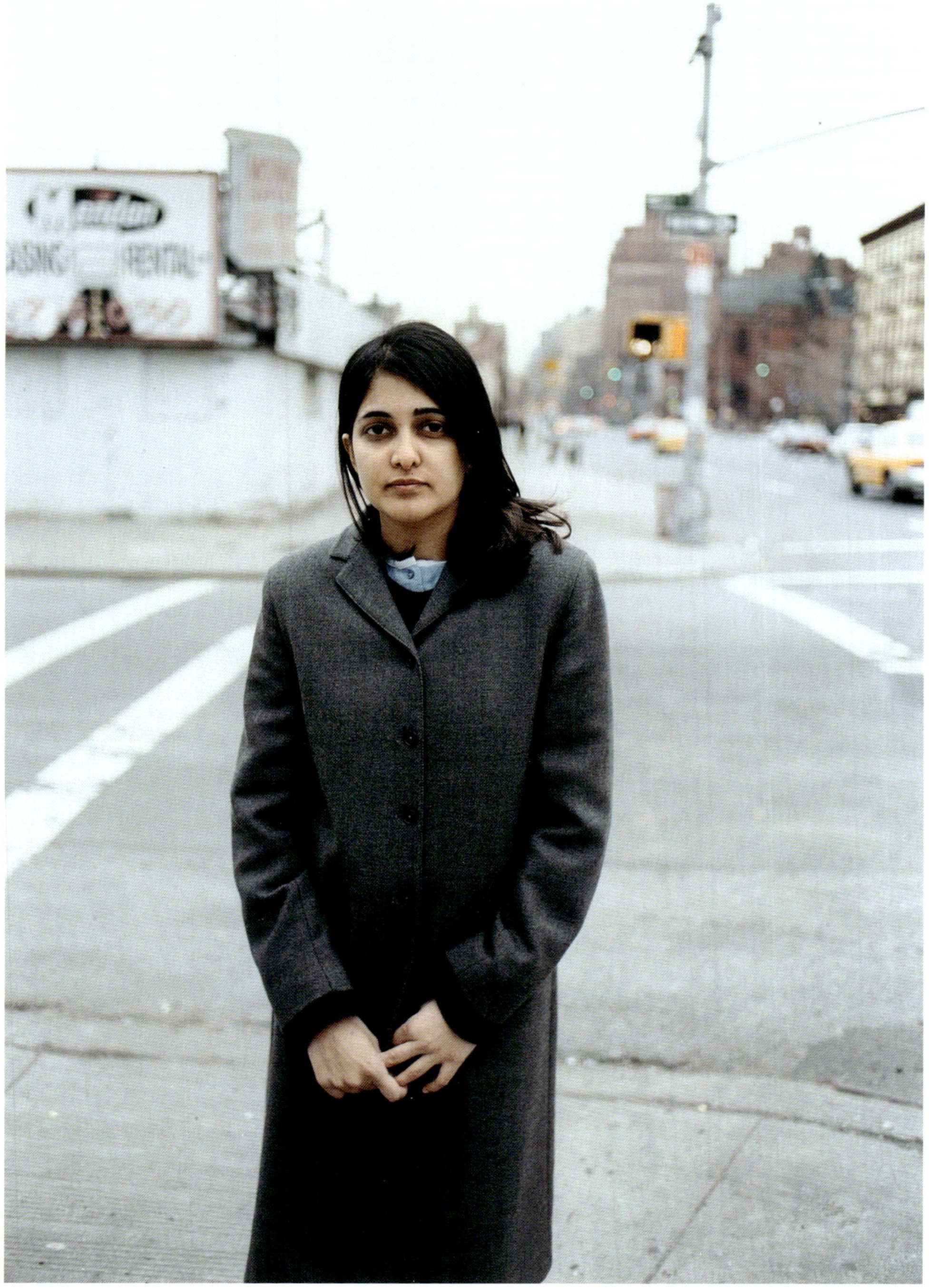

15 MERIDEL RUBENSTEIN *Peggy Martinez, Santa Cruz, '64 Chevy Two-Tone* 1980

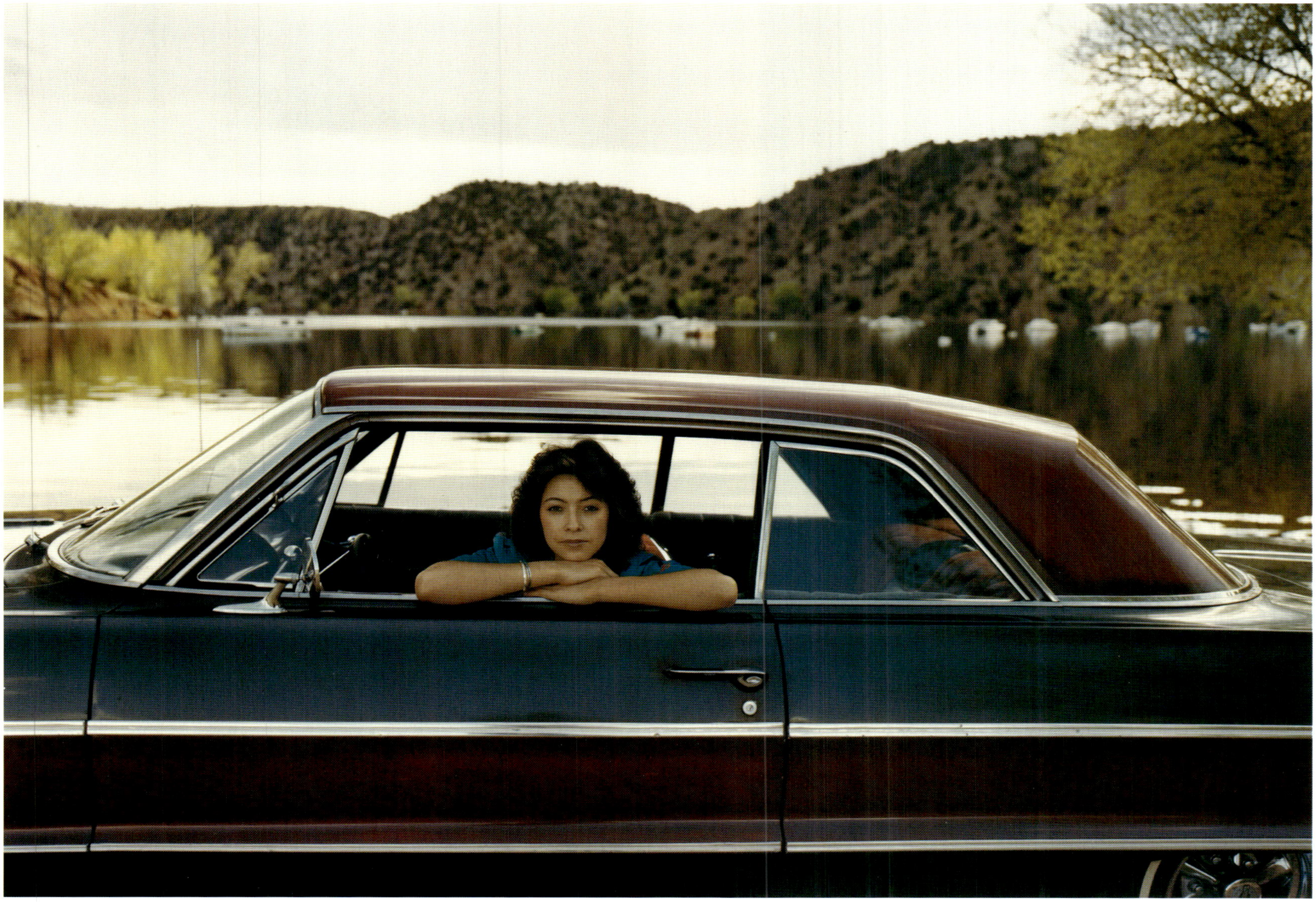

16 DAVID HILLIARD *Dad* 1998

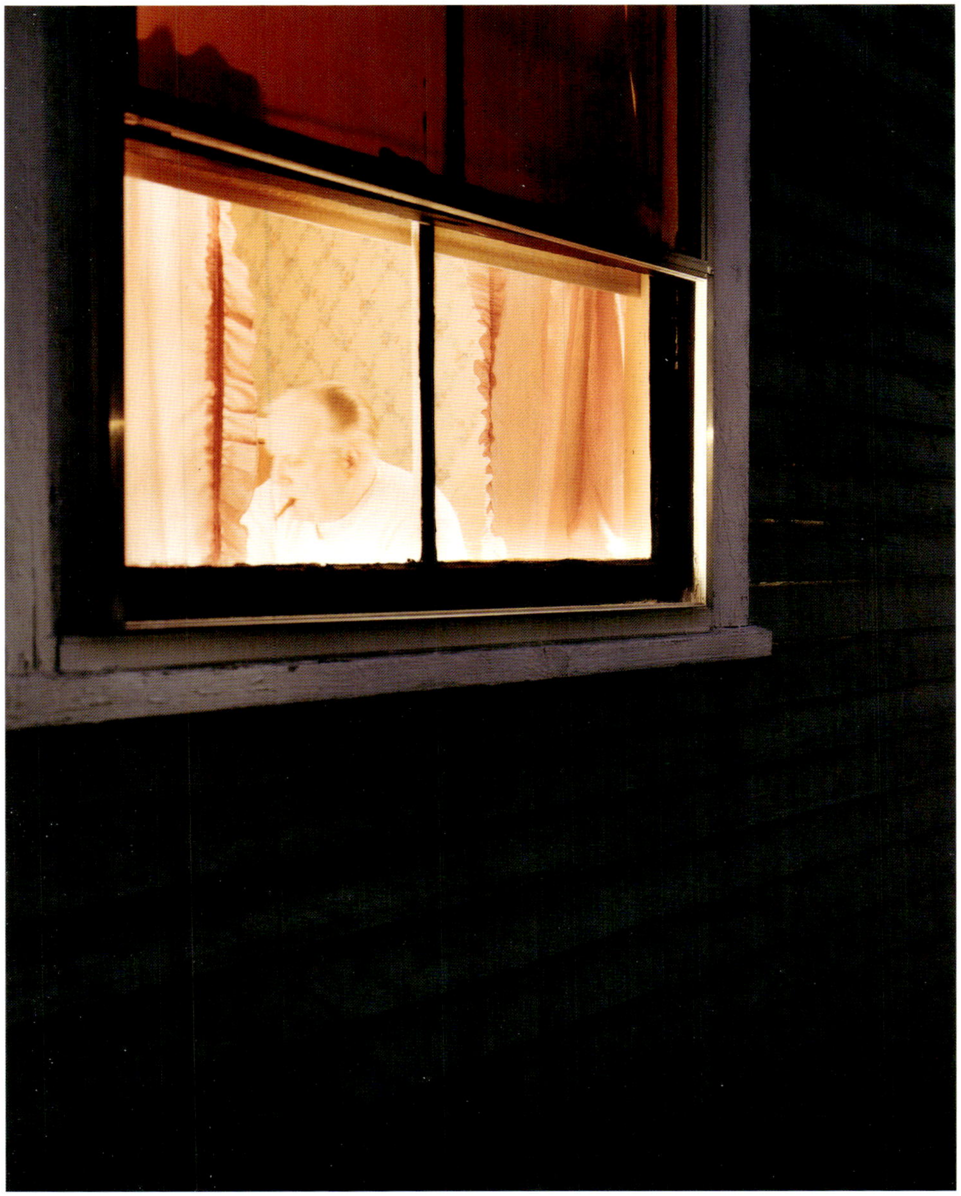

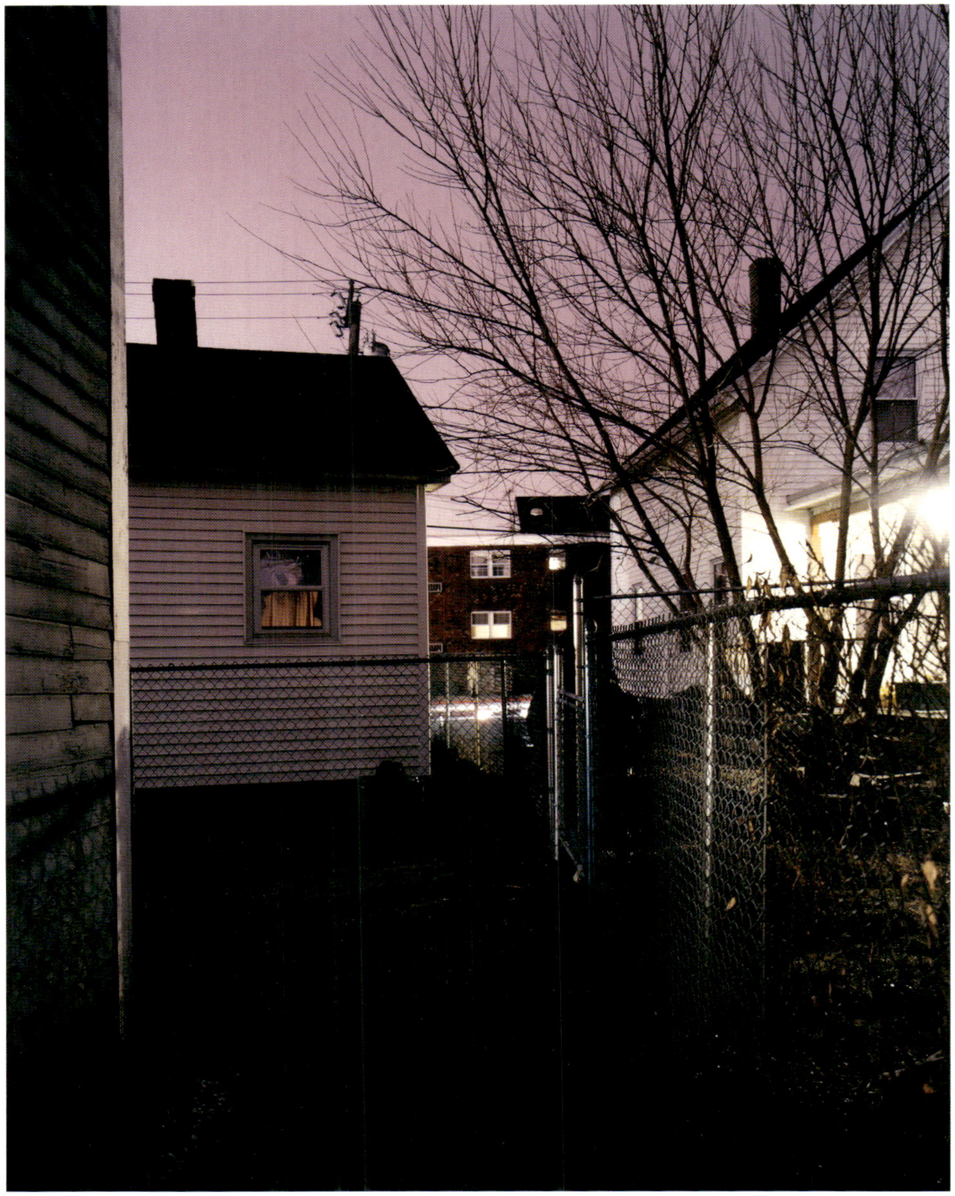

17 ROY DECARAVA *Sam and Shirley Talking* 1952

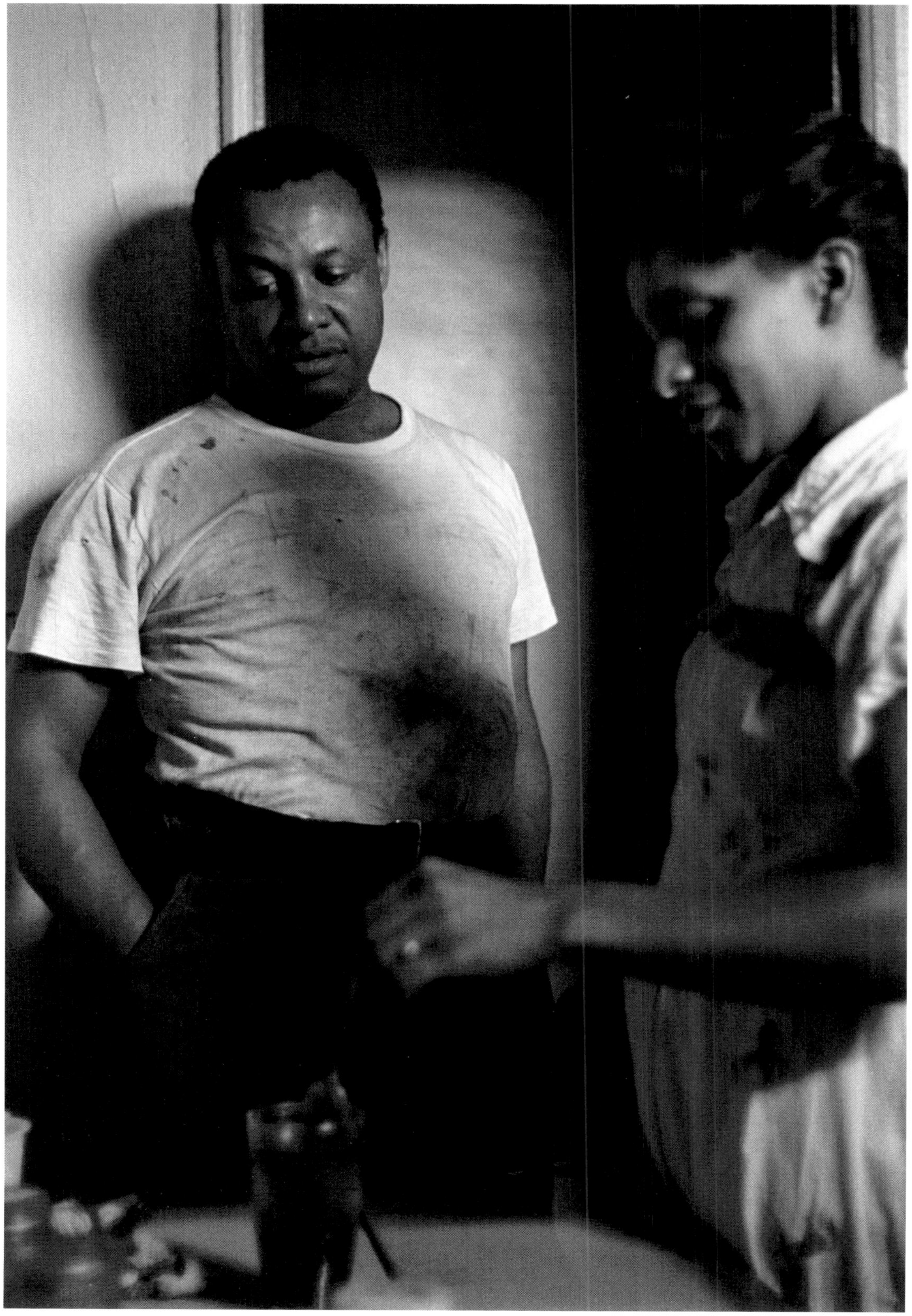

18 LARRY SULTAN *The Green Wall* 1989

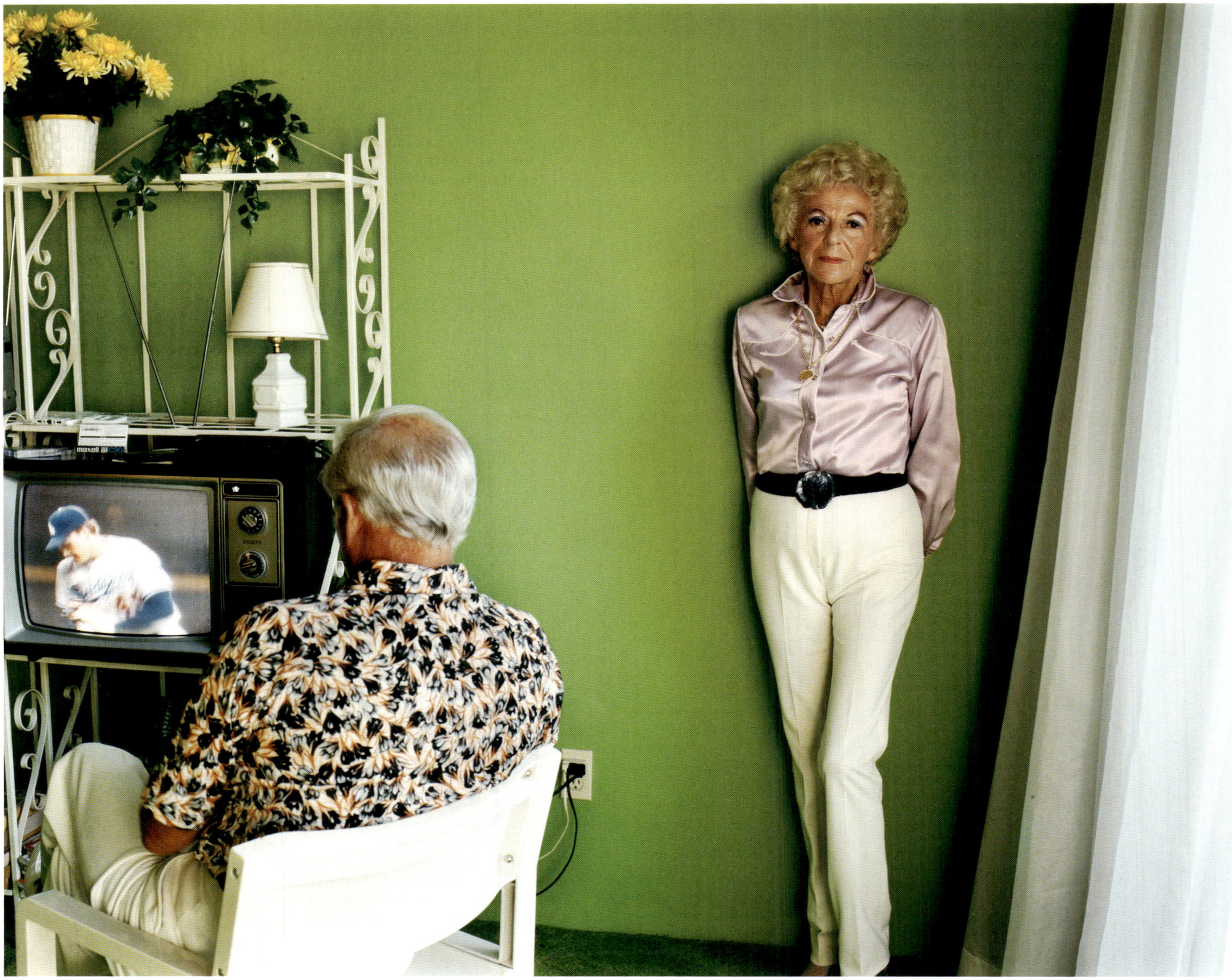

19 THOMAS STRUTH *The Richter Family I, Cologne, 2002* 2002

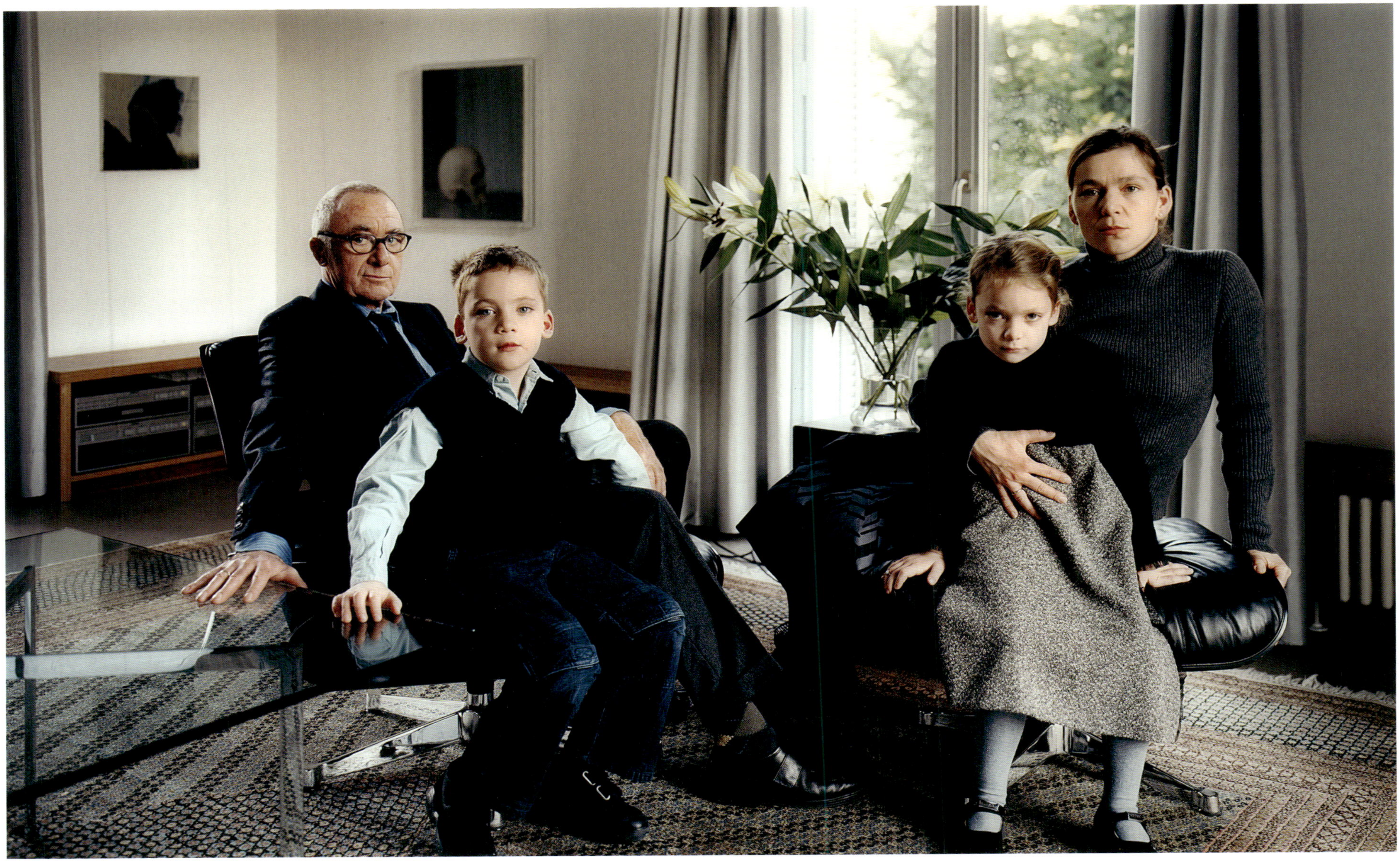

20 TINA BARNEY *Father and Sons* 1996

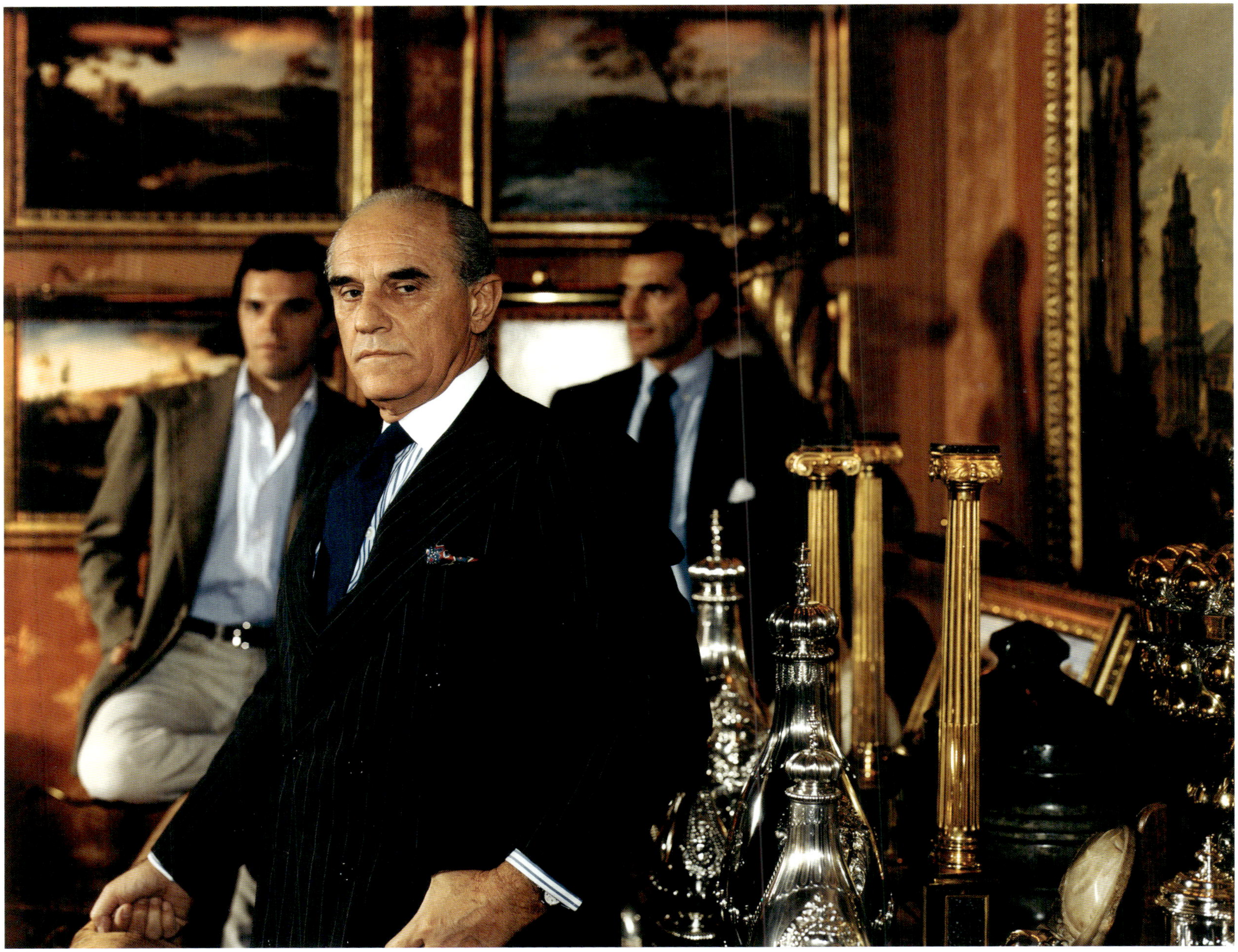

21 CARRIE MAE WEEMS *After Manet* 2001

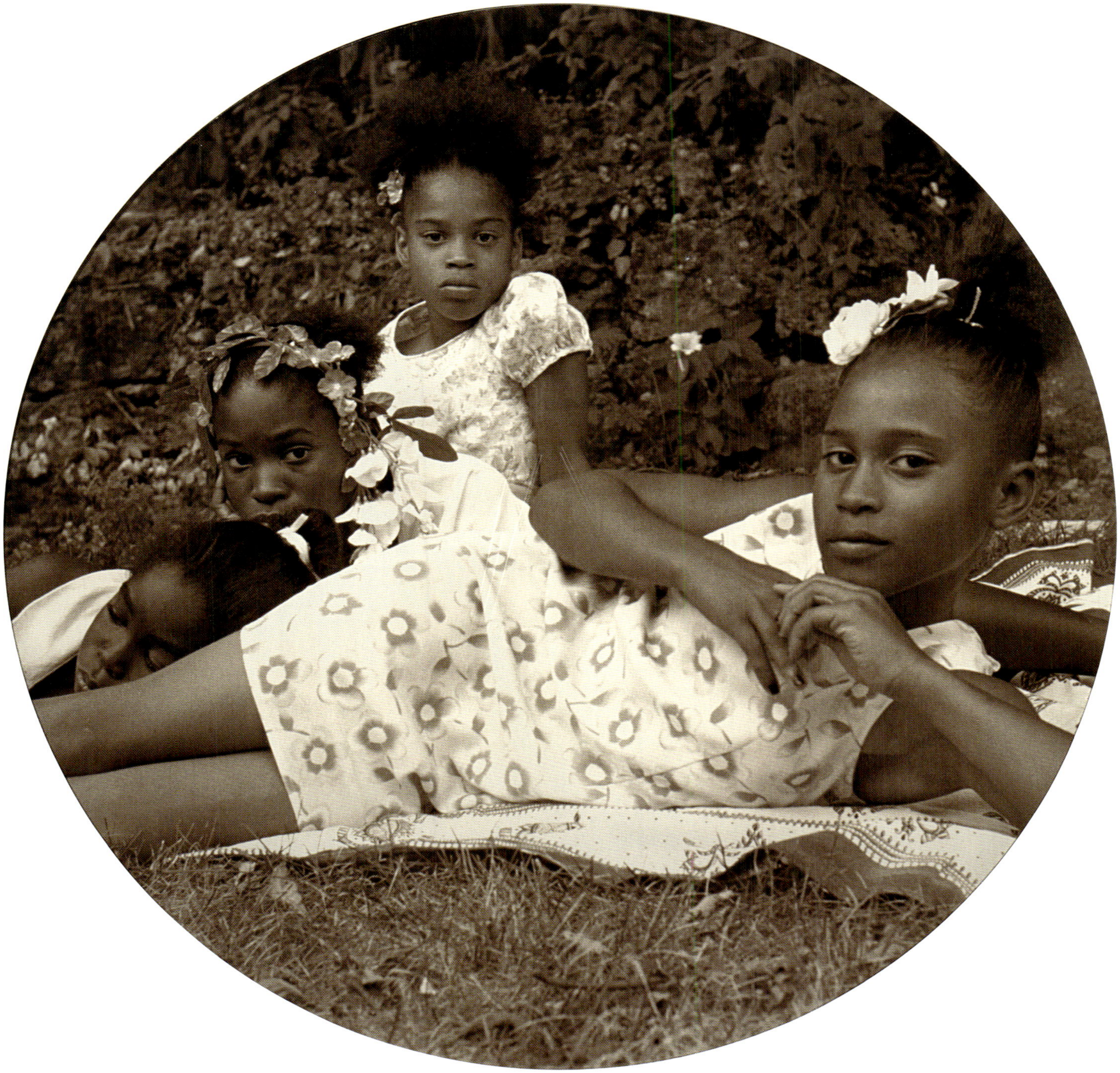

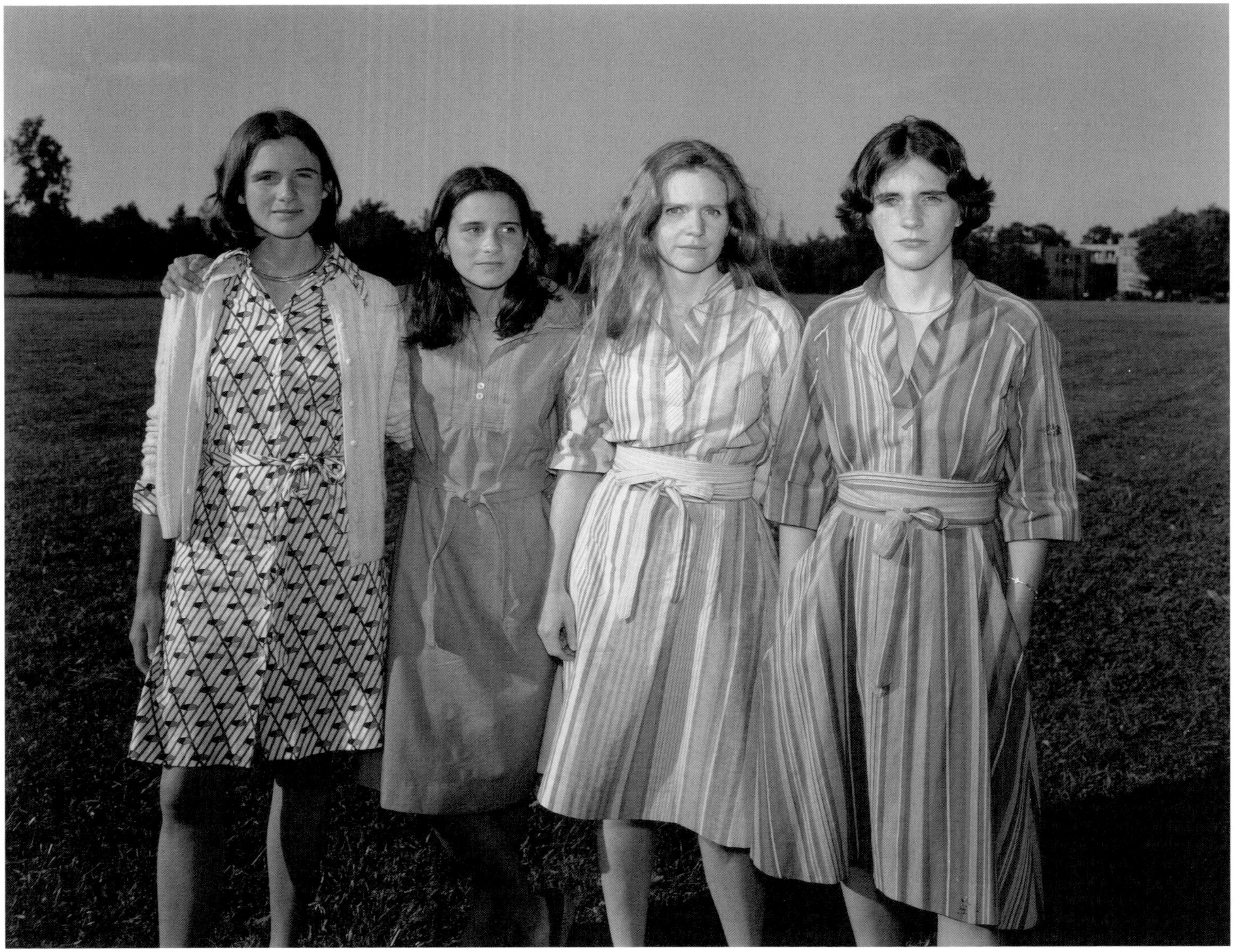

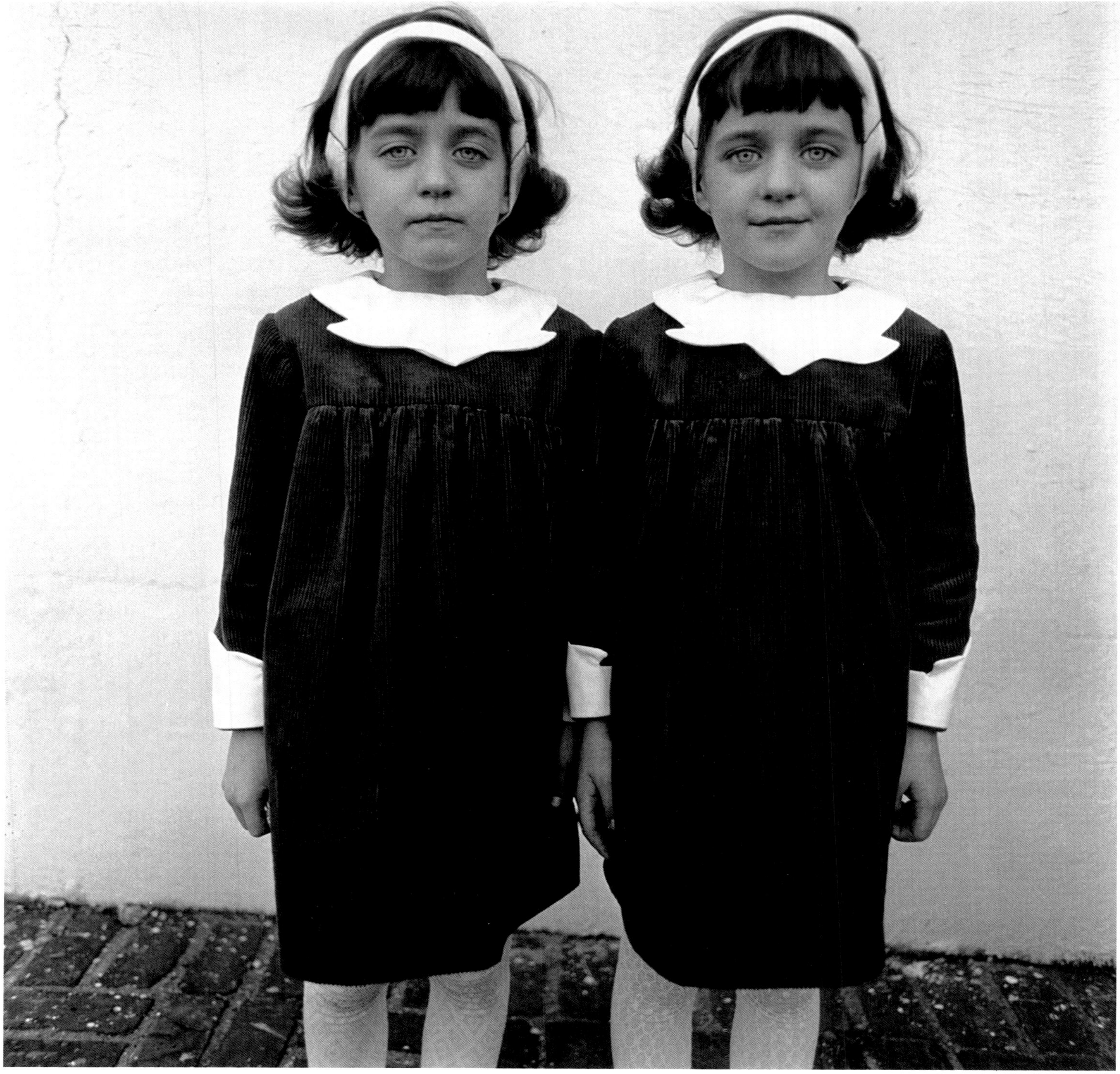

25 MIKE DISFARMER *Untitled (Willie Dettweiler, Vernon Higgs, Heber Springs, Arkansas)* 1946

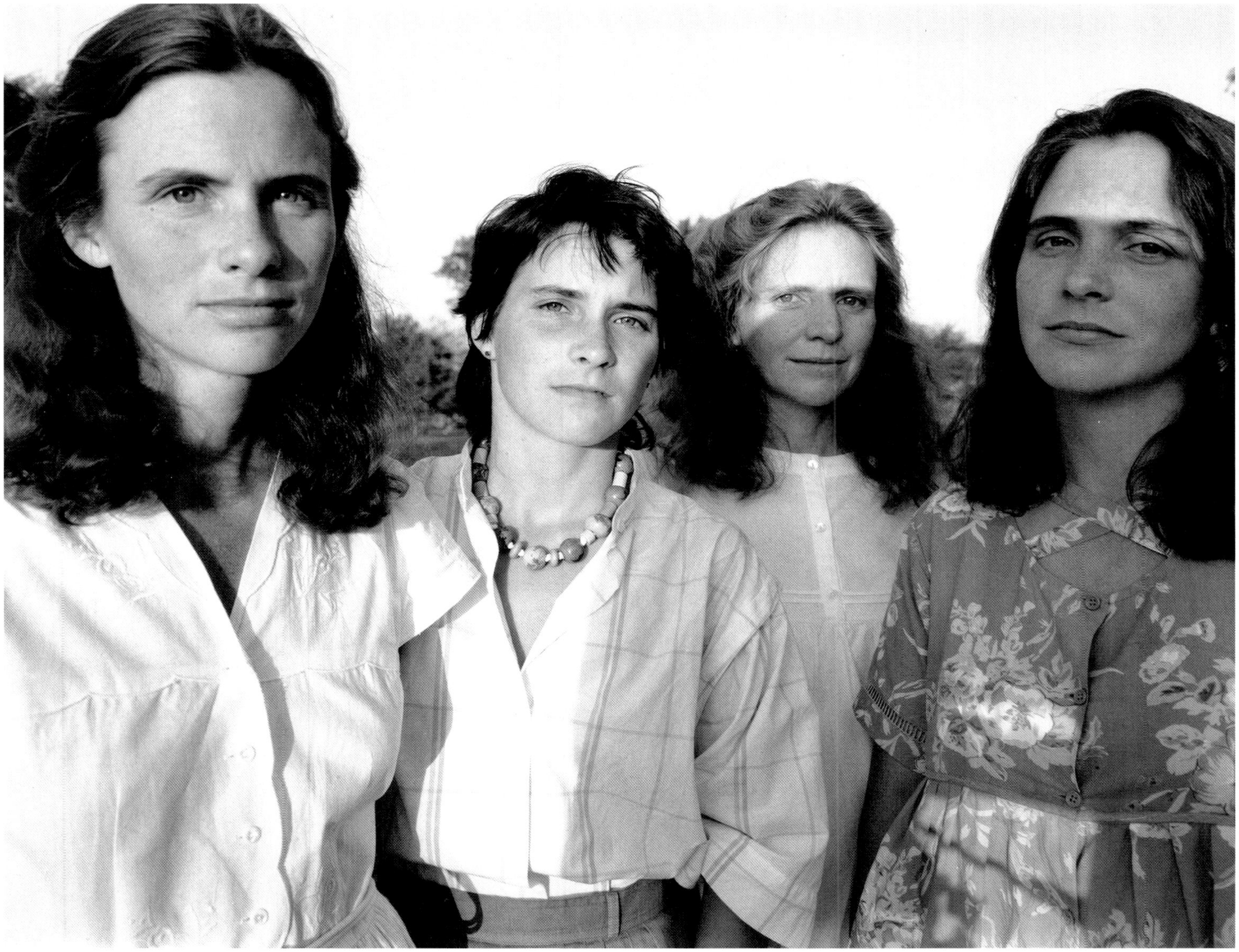

(PREVIOUS PAGE) 22 NICHOLAS NIXON *Heather Brown McCann, Mimi Brown, Bebe Brown Nixon, Laurie Brown, Hartford, Conn., 1976* 1976

23 NICHOLAS NIXON *Heather Brown, Mimi Brown, Bebe Brown Nixon, Laurie Brown Tranchin, Brighton, Mass., 1983* 1983

(OPPOSITE PAGE) 24 DIANE ARBUS *Identical Twins, Roselle, N.J.* 1967

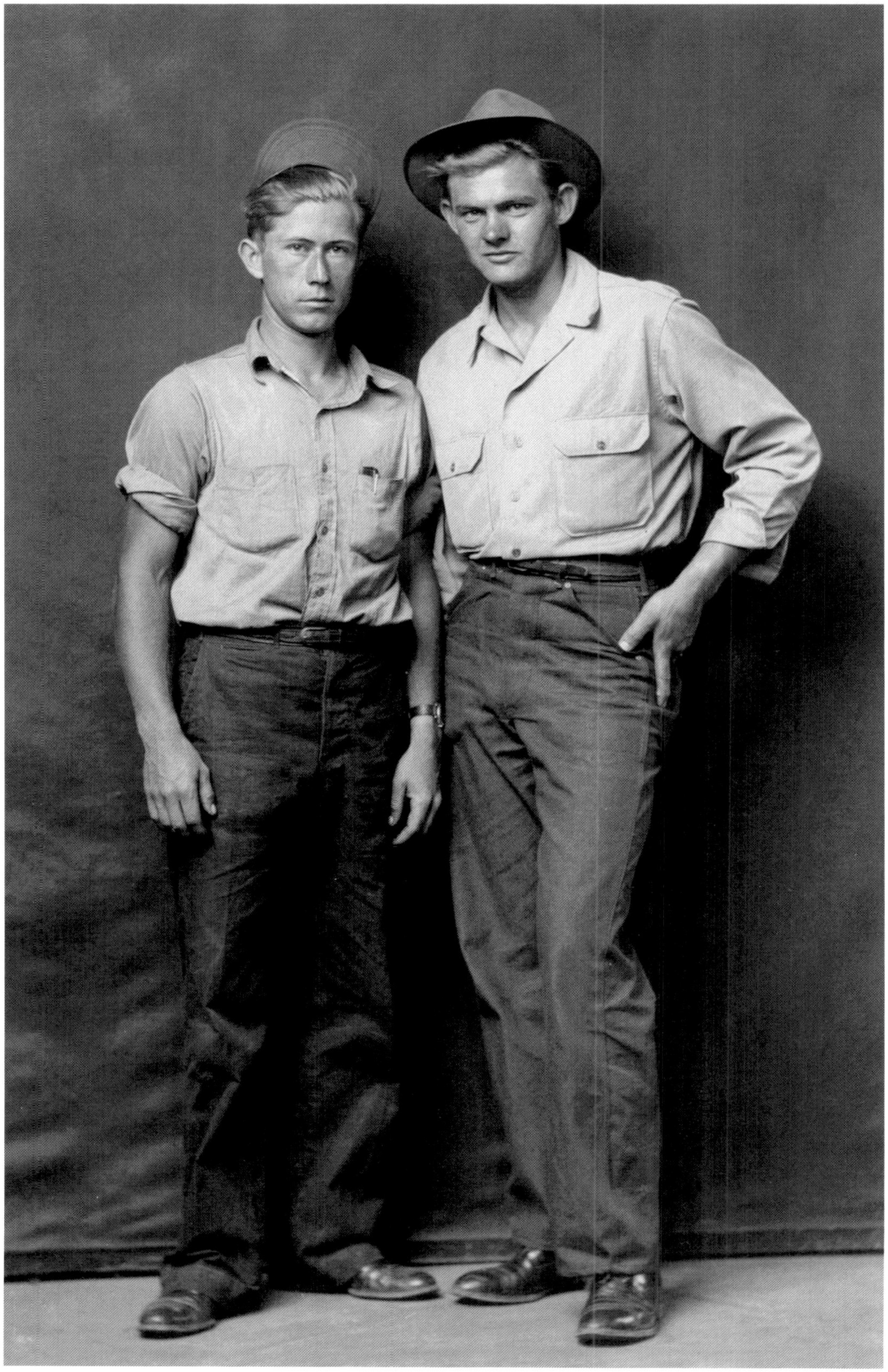

26 AUGUST SANDER *Boxers* 1929

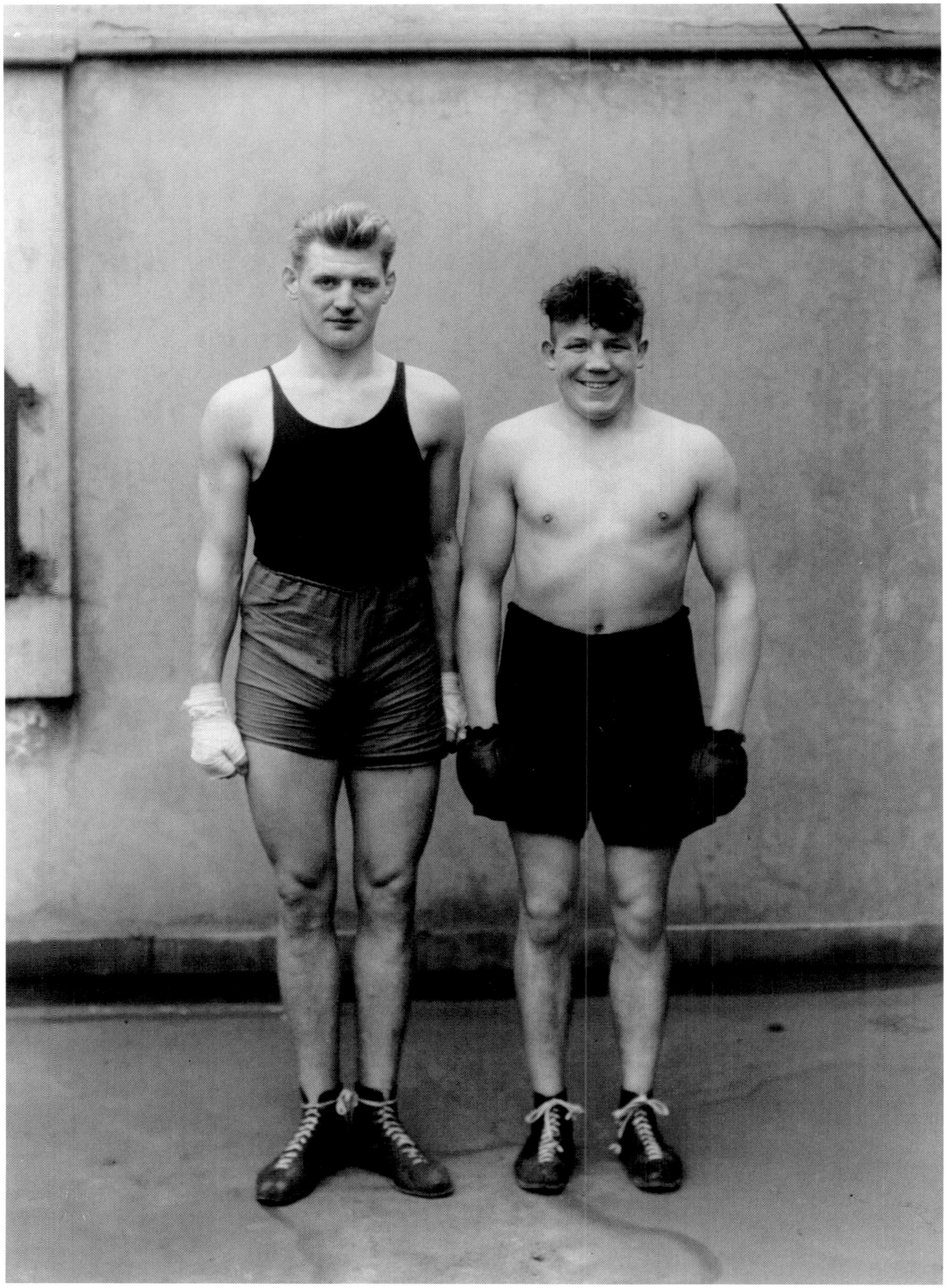

27 CHAN CHAO *Mya Khaing, May 1997* 1997

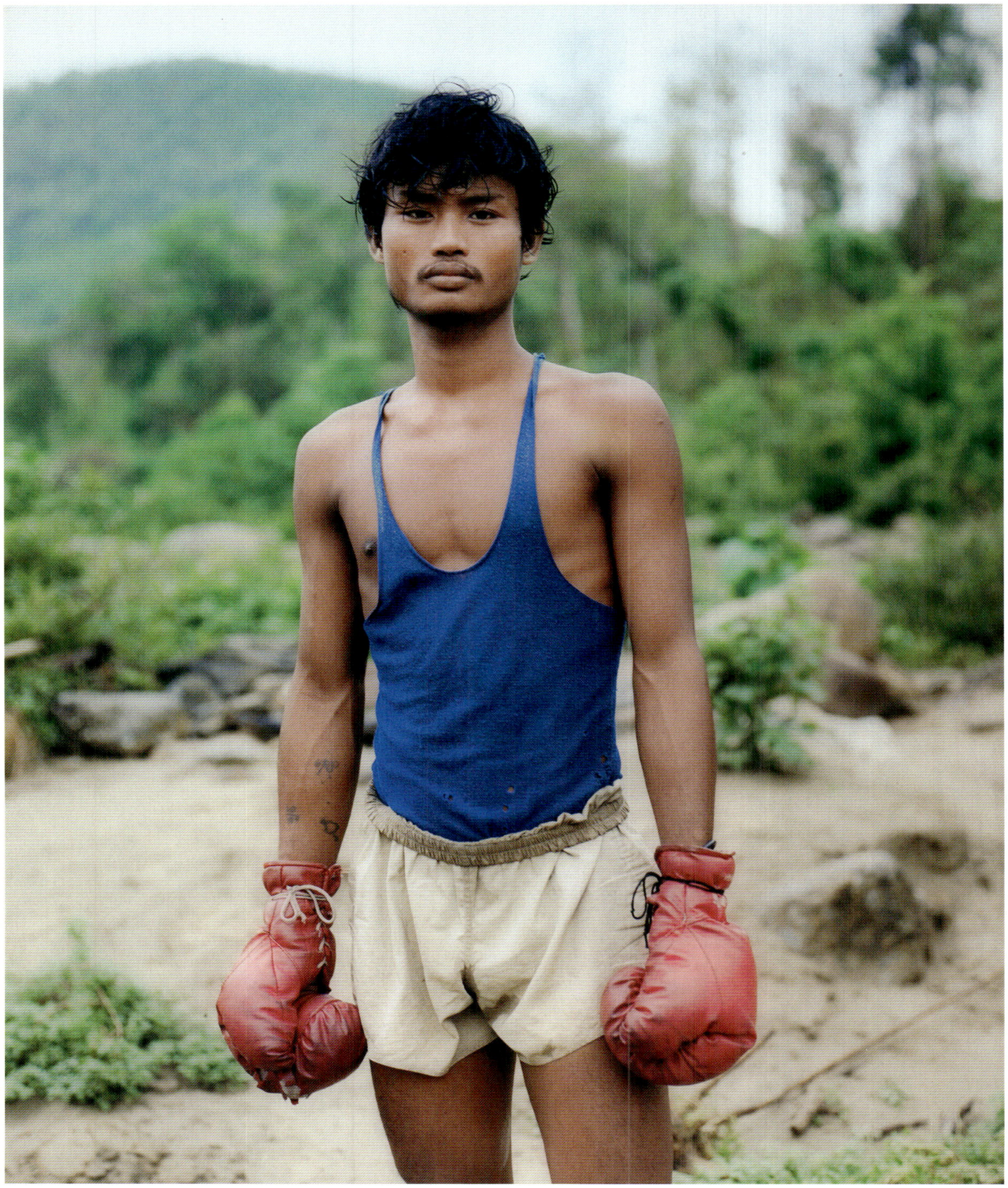

 Omirzo Salomov, 36 years old, Tajik: Engineer, Romish restaurant 2001

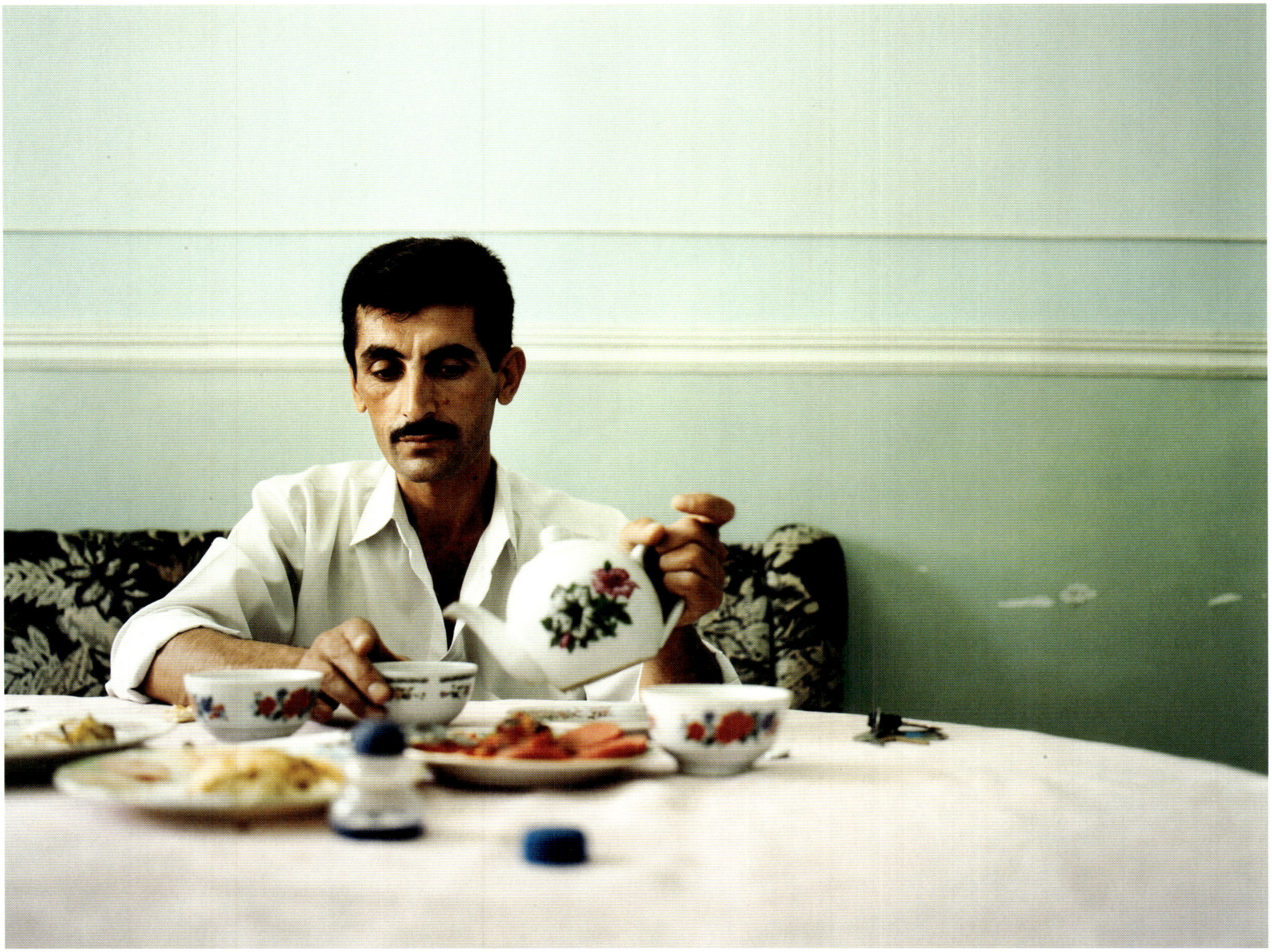

29 STEPHEN SHORE *Ginger Shore, Miami, Florida, November 12, 1977* 1977

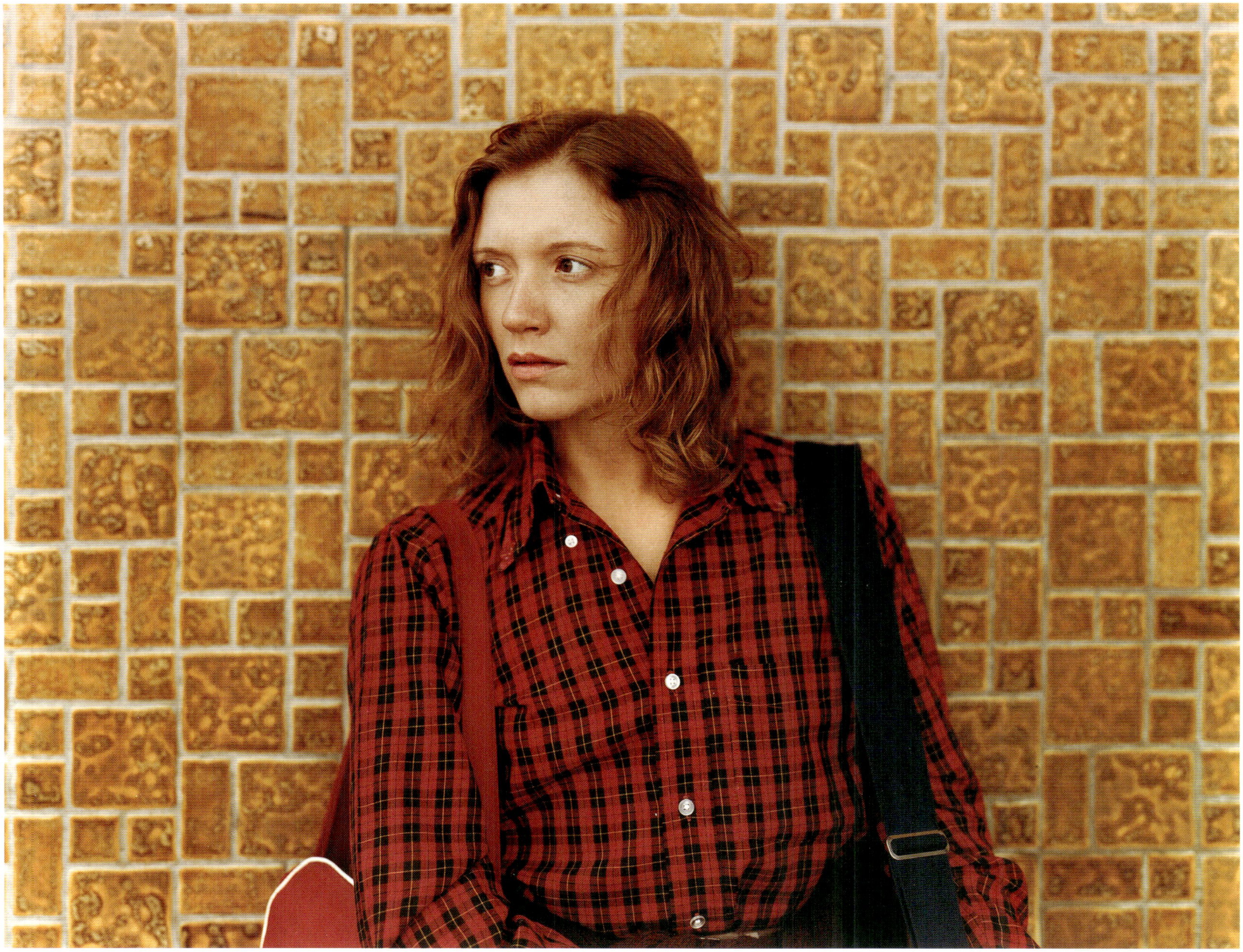

30 DAVID HOCKNEY *Billy Wilder lighting his cigar, Dec. 1982* 1982

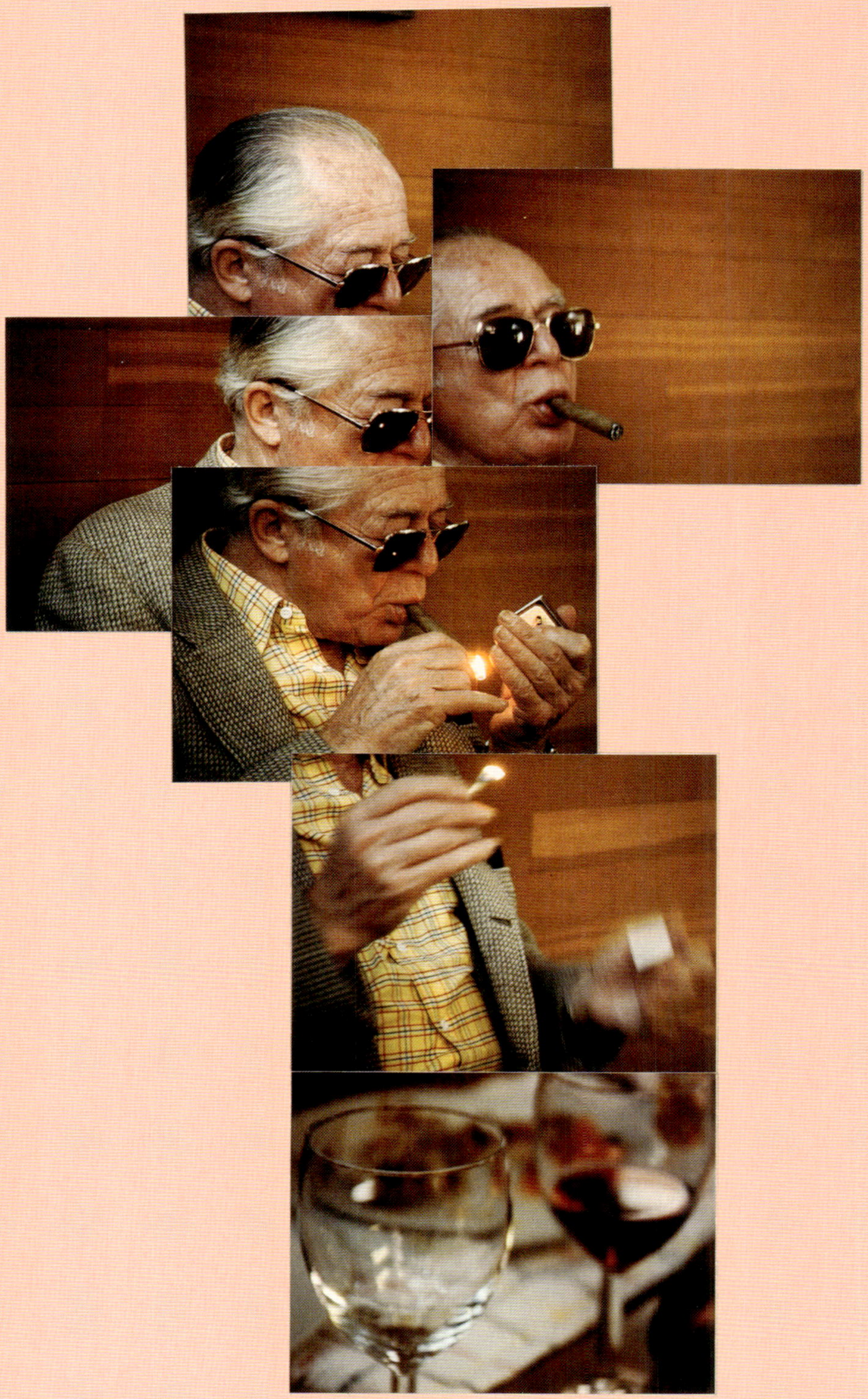

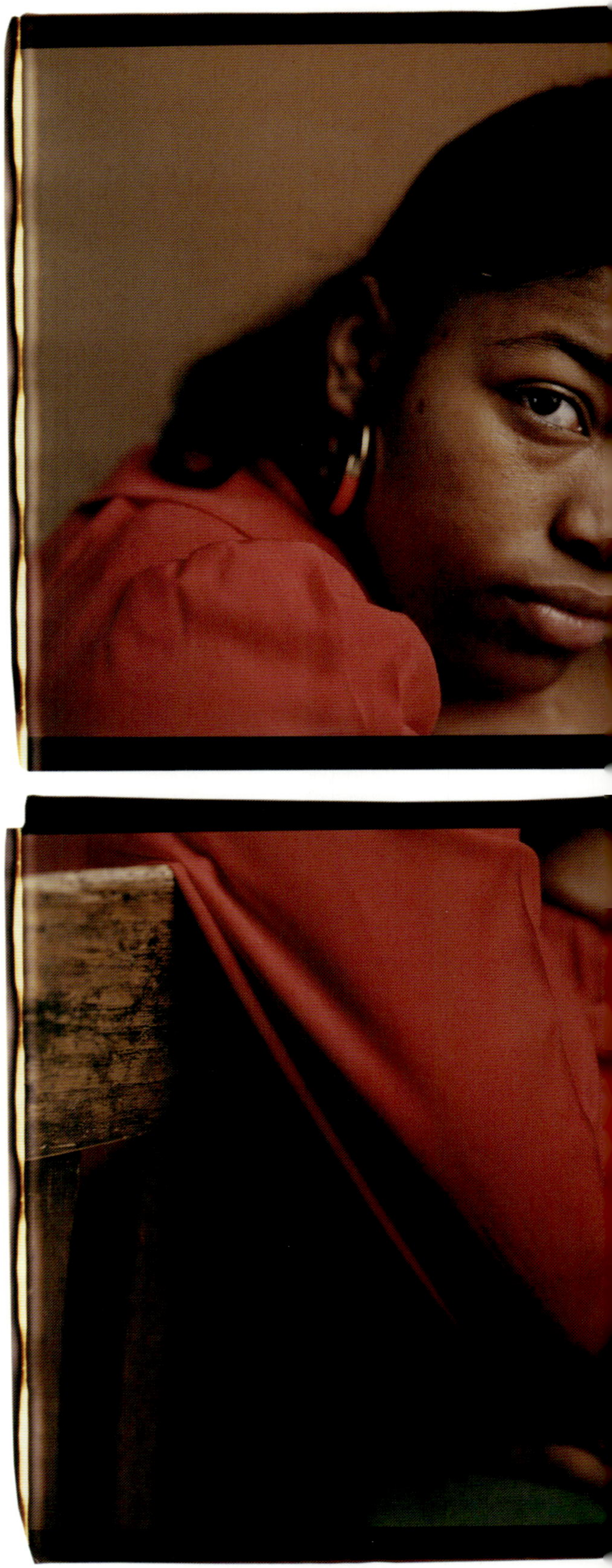

31 DAWOUD BEY *Toyia, Kelvin & Erica II* 1993

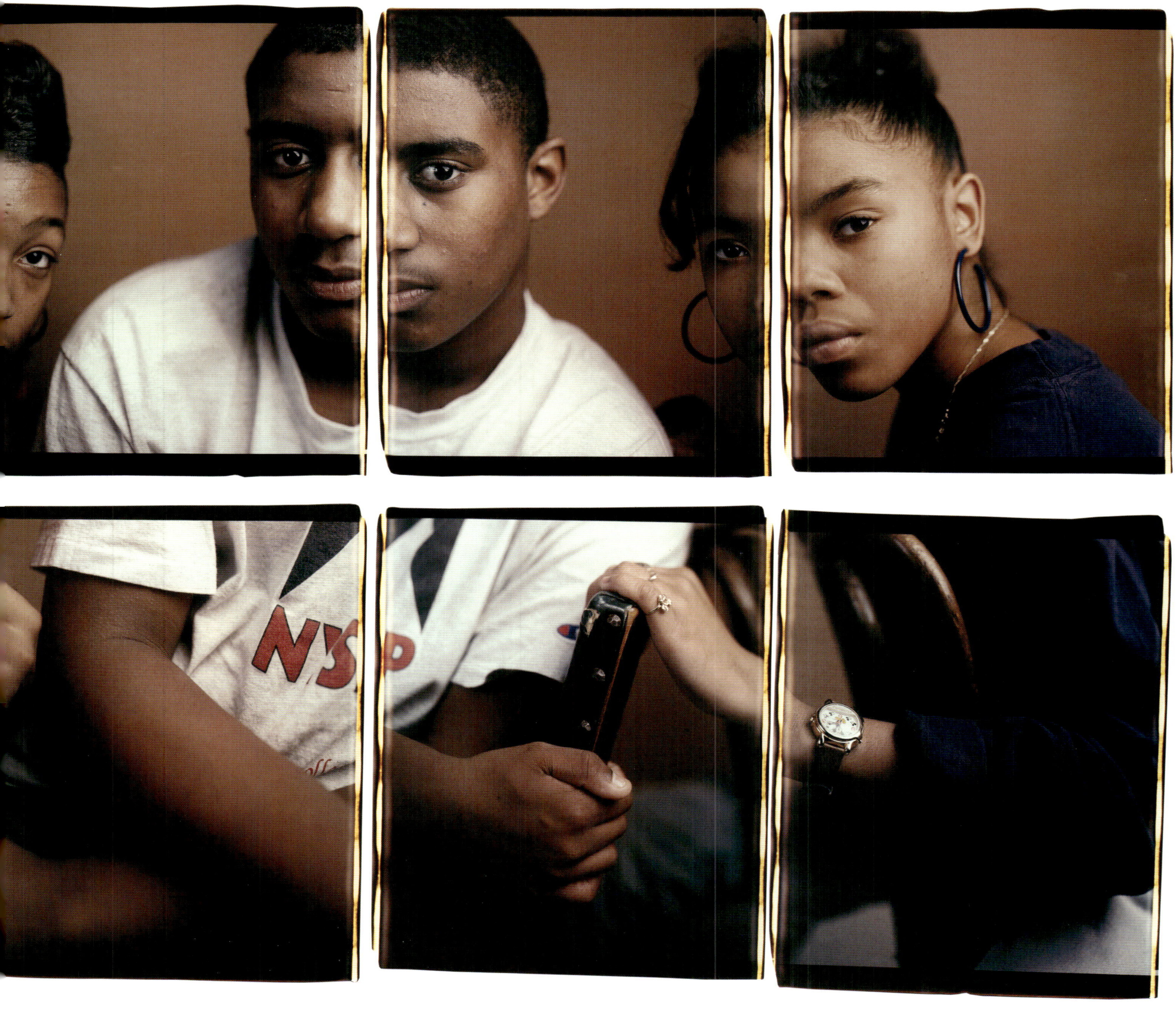

 BEN GEST *Chuck, Alice and Dale* 2003

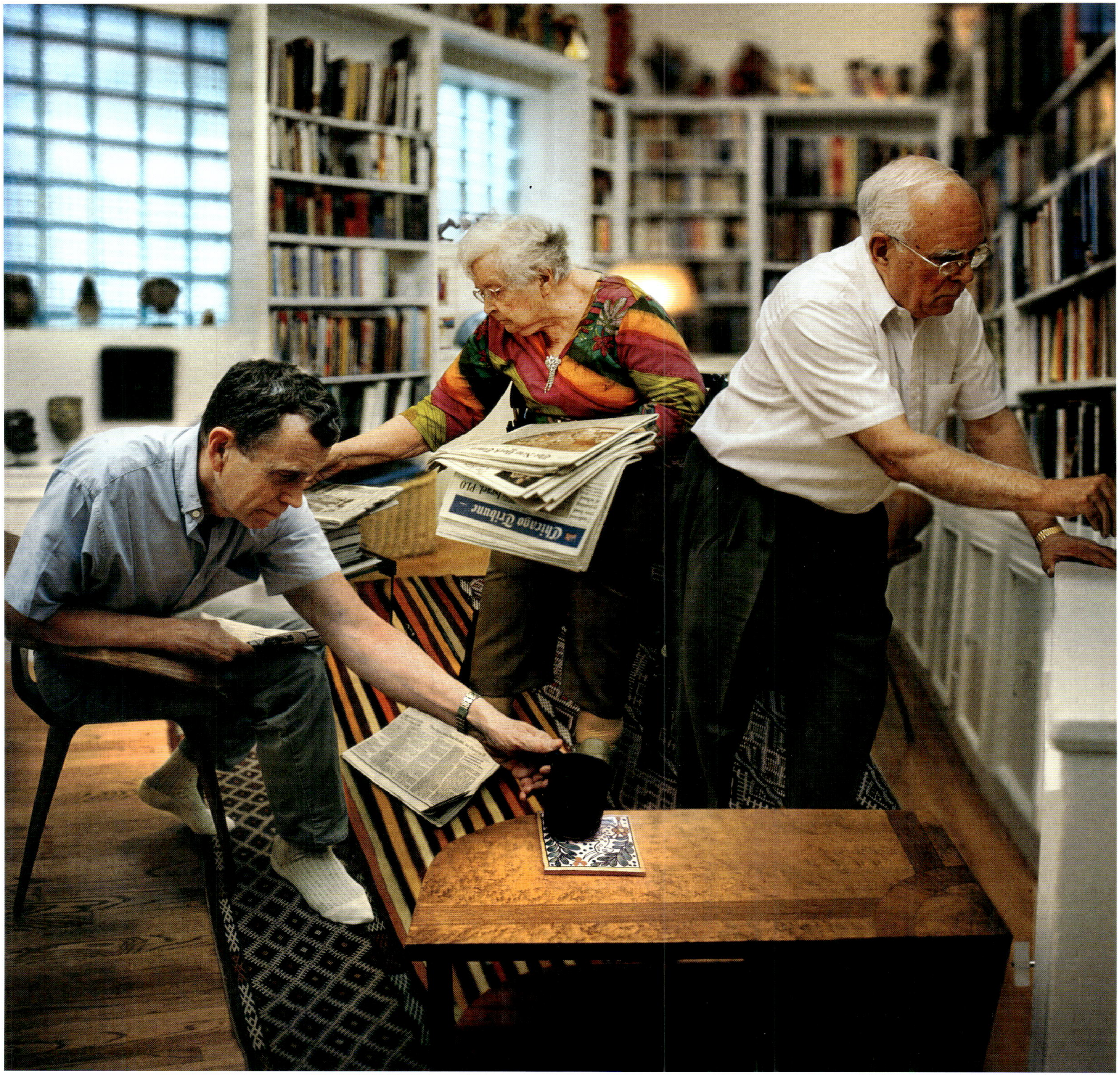
Chicago Tribune

33 PHILIP-LORCA DICORCIA *Mario* 1978

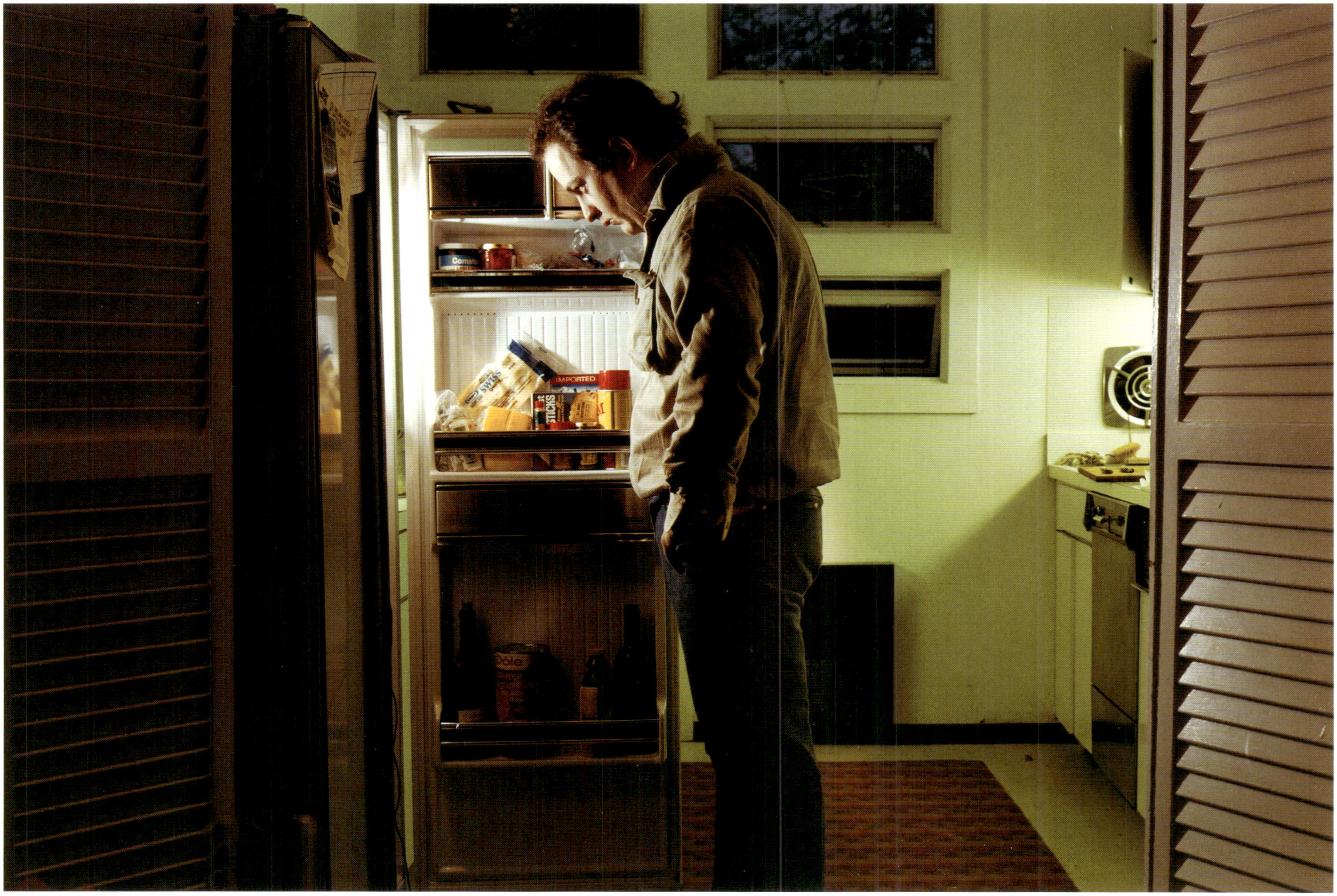
IMPORTED
Dole

34 EDWARD WESTON *Johan Hagemeyer, 1925* 1925

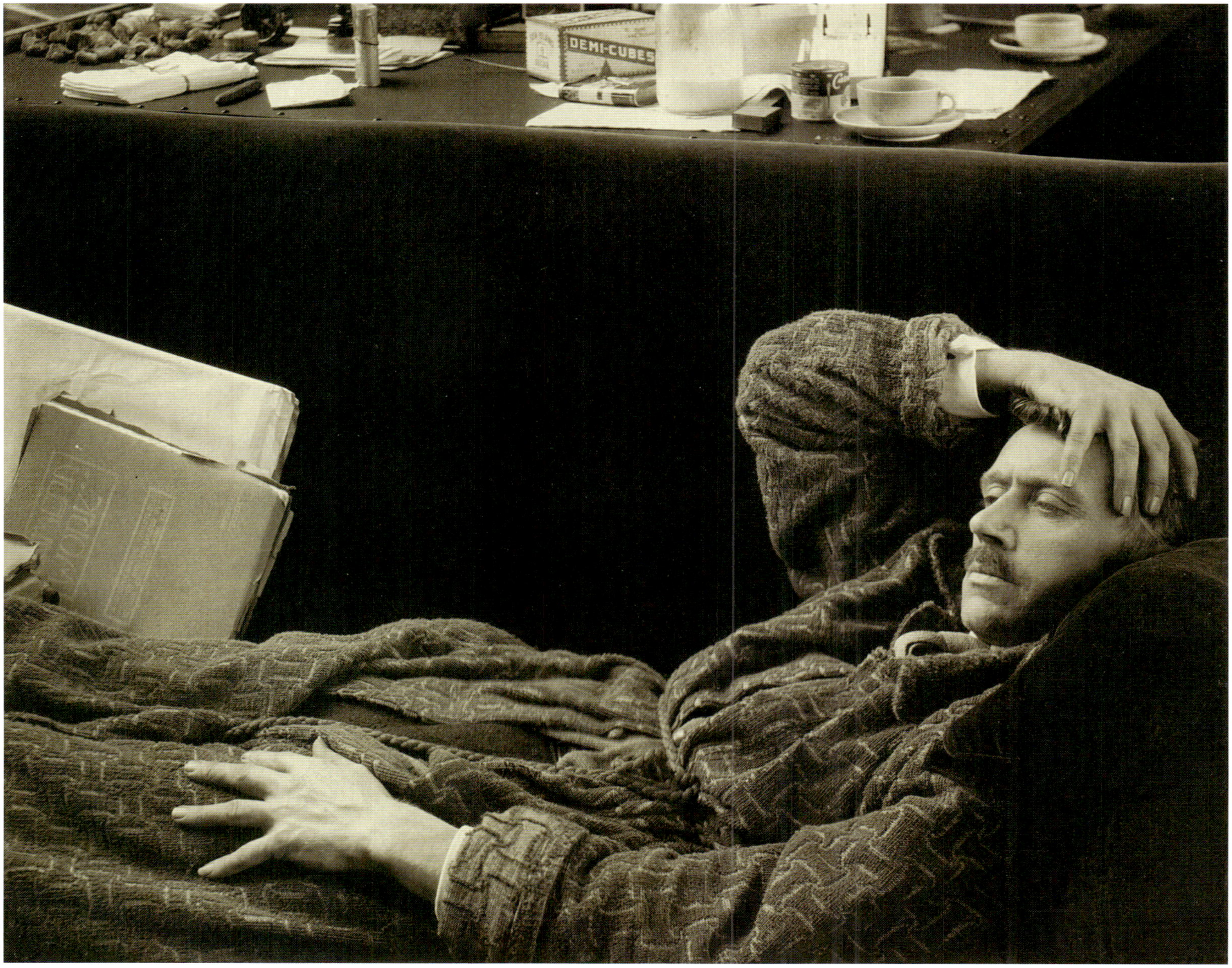
DEMI-CUBES

35 HENRI CARTIER-BRESSON *Washington, D.C. (Robert Kennedy)* 1961

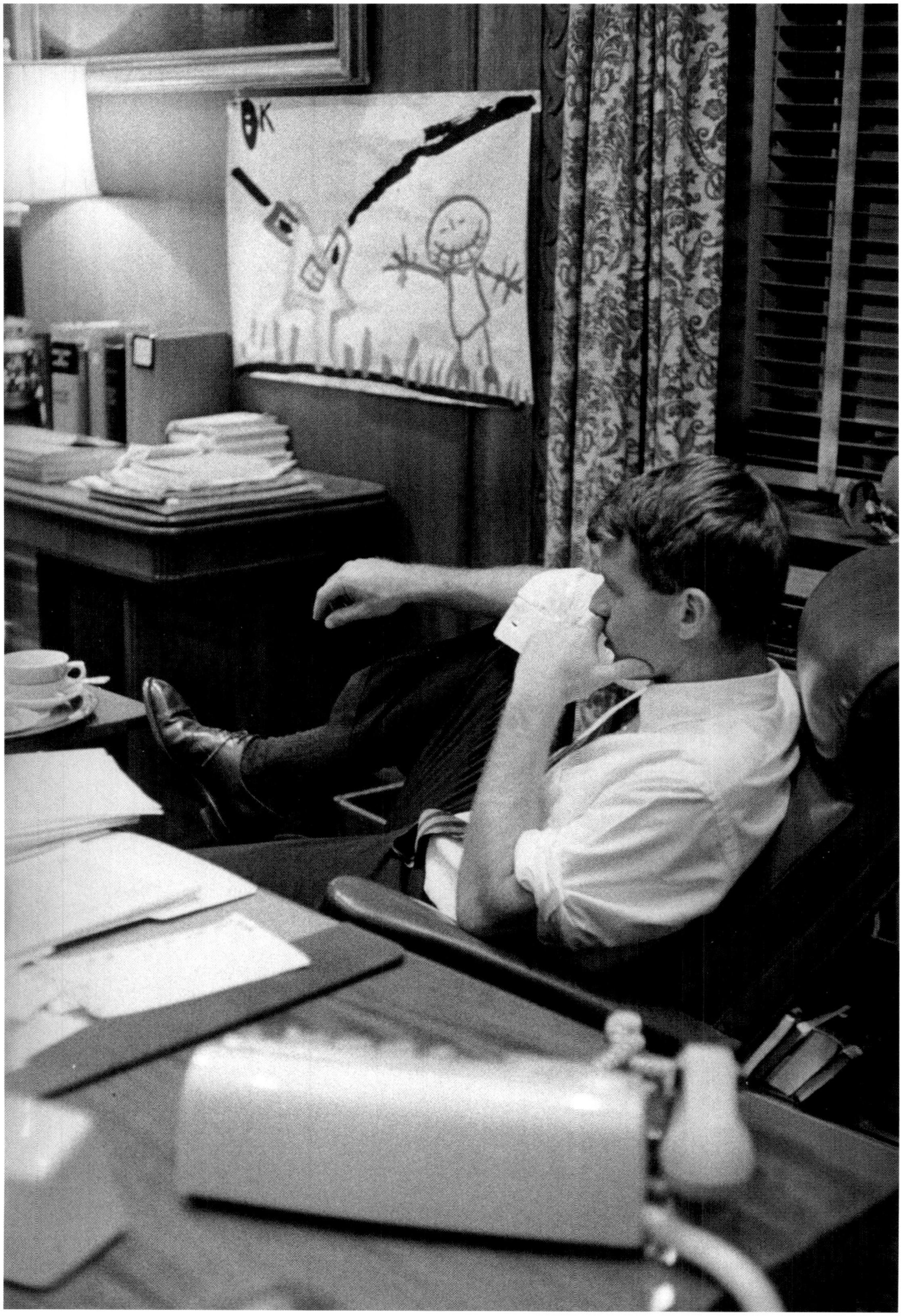

36 PHILIPPE HALSMANN *Richard M. Nixon* 1955

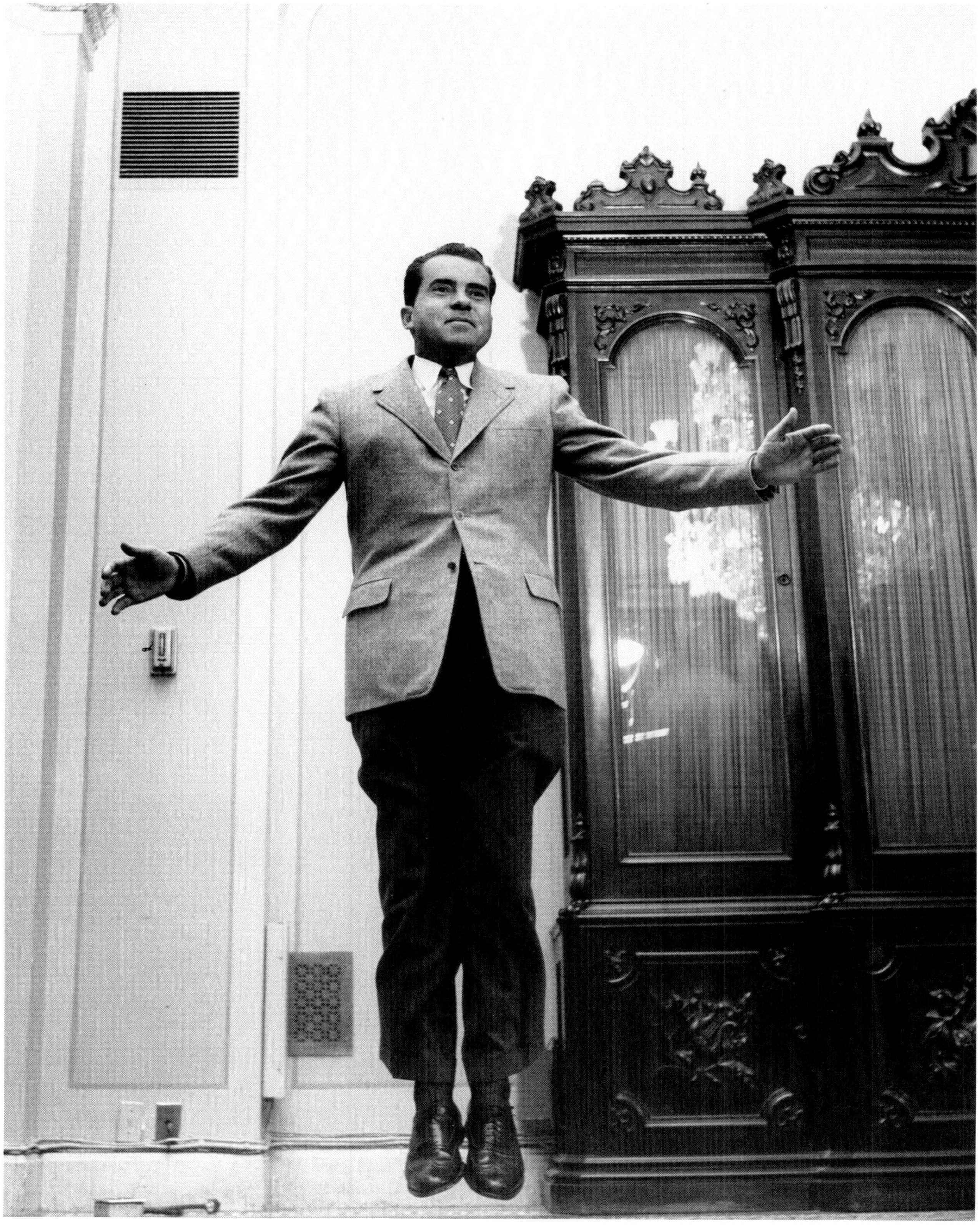

37 TINA BARNEY *Entrance Hall* 1996

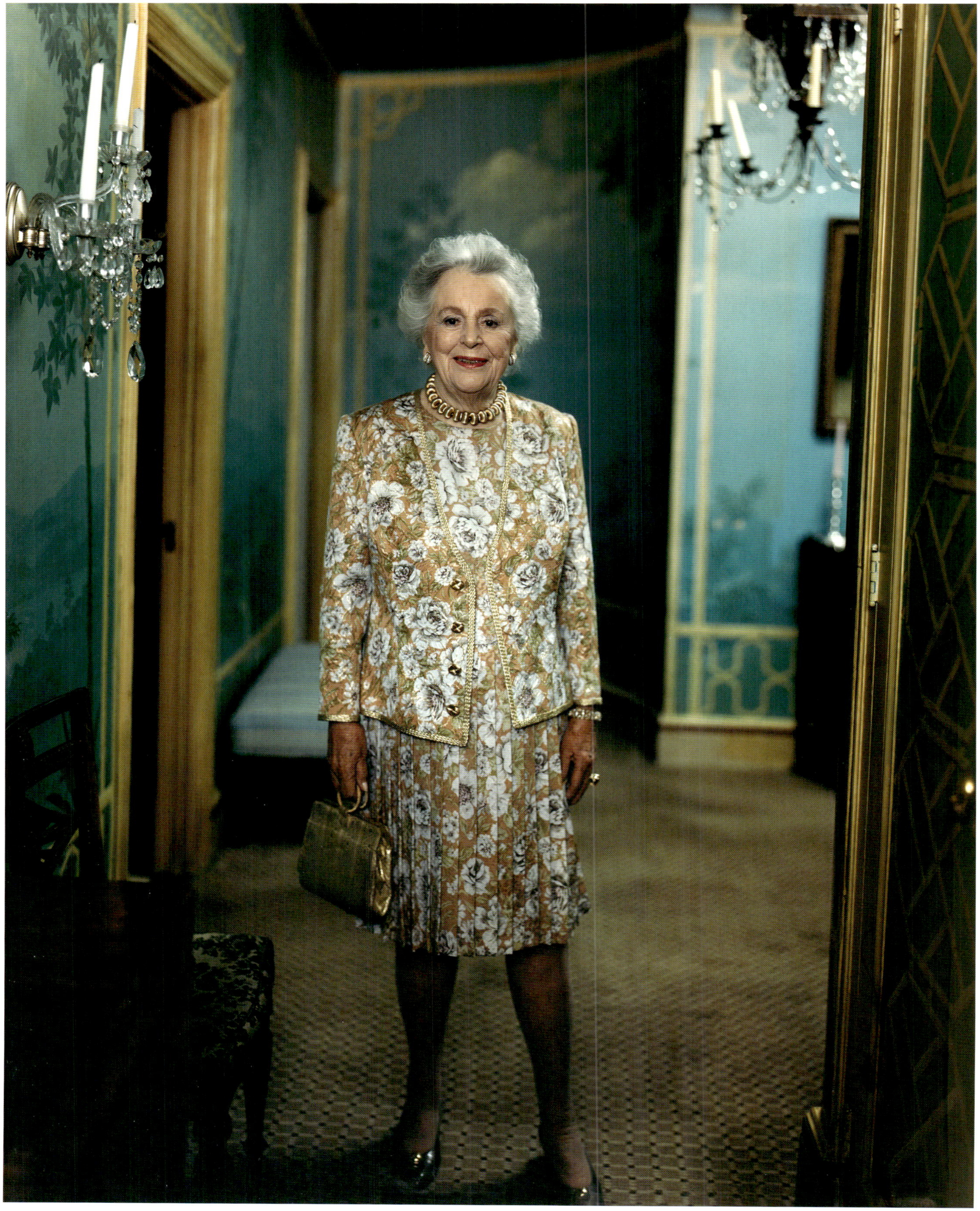

38 MANUEL ALVAREZ BRAVO *Frida Kahlo in Manuel Alvarez Bravo's Studio* 1930s

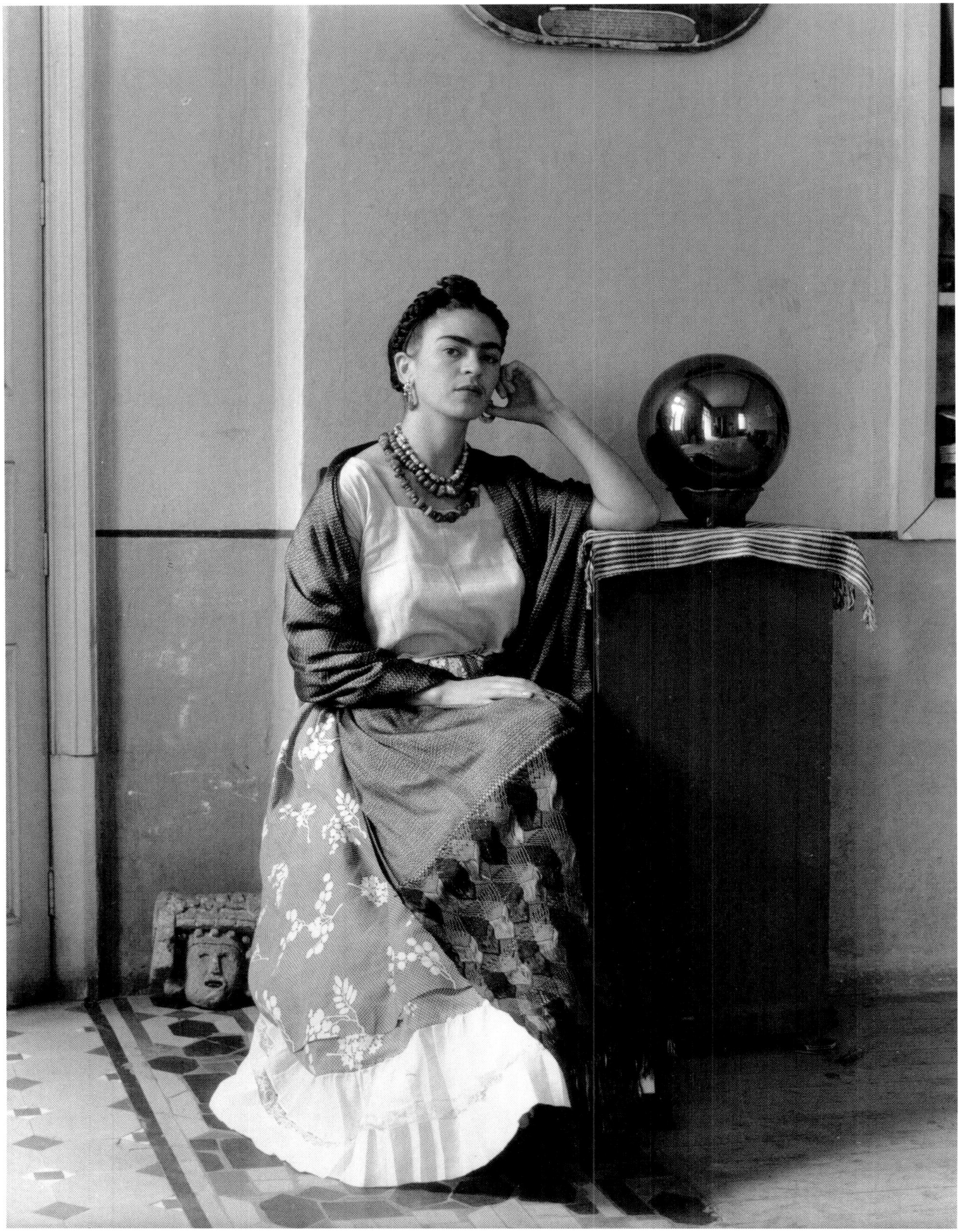

39 CHUCK STEWART *Eric Dolphy, New York City, February 1964* 1964

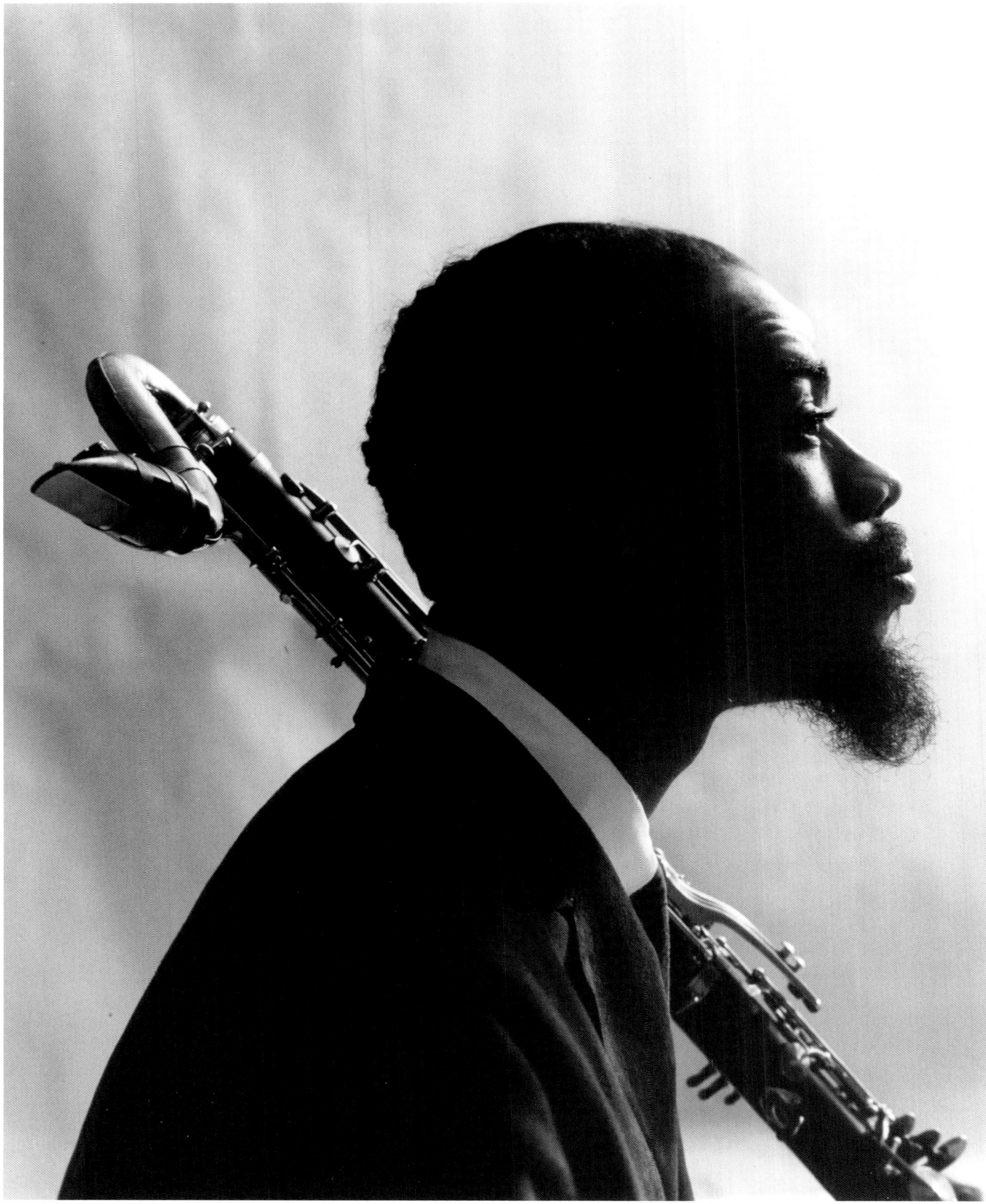

40 DIETER APPELT *The Mark on the Mirror Breathing Makes* 1978

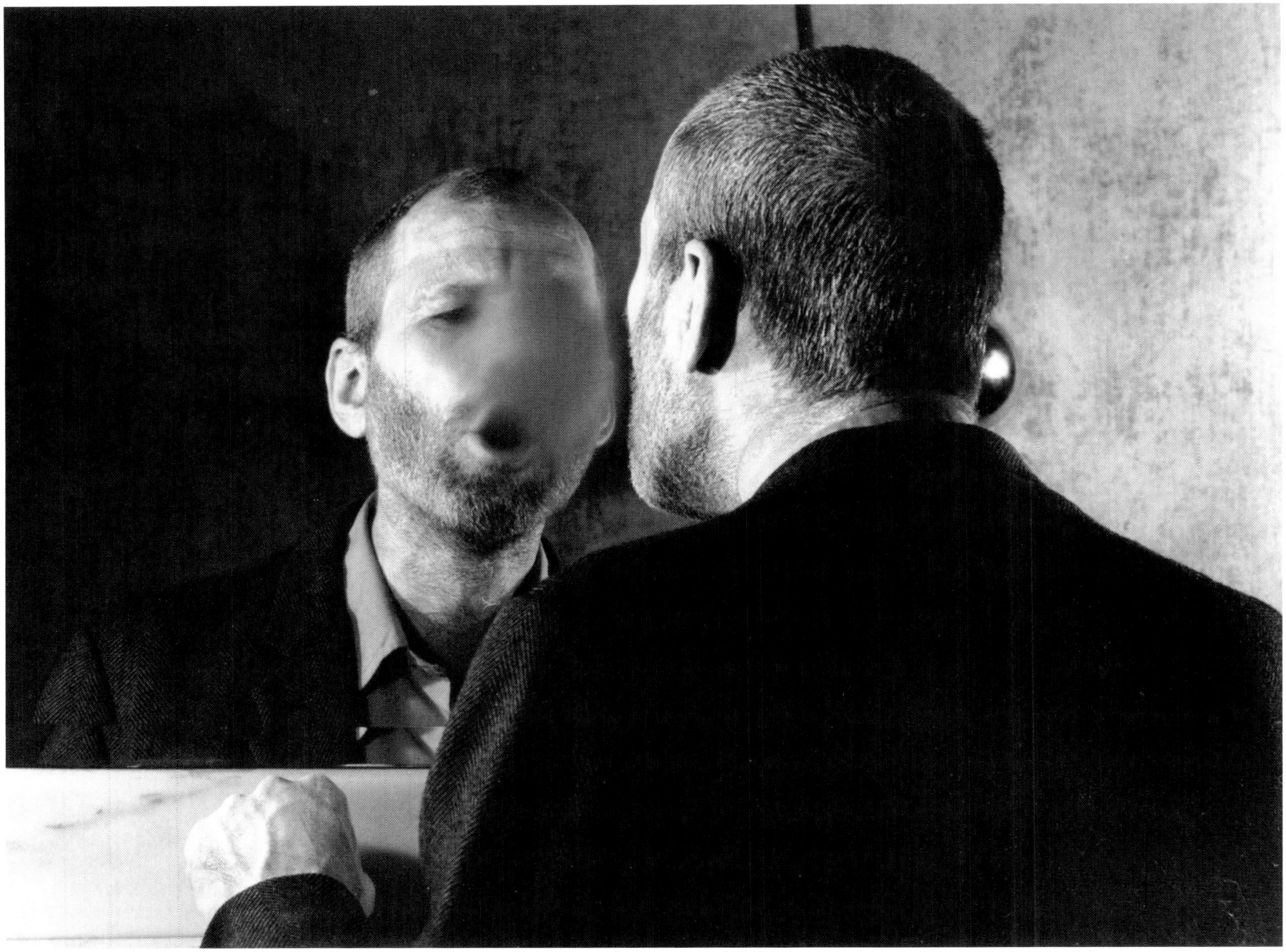

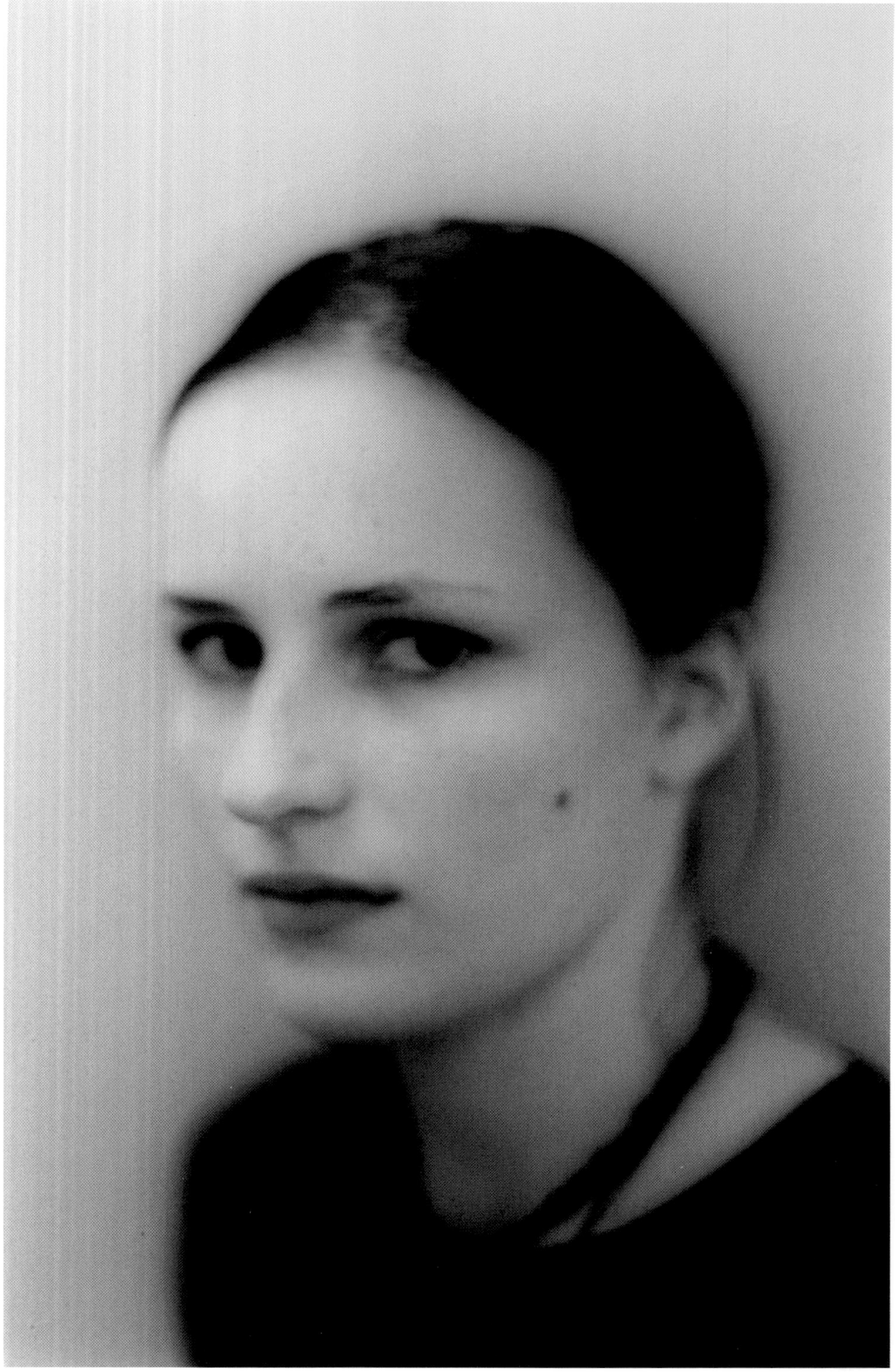

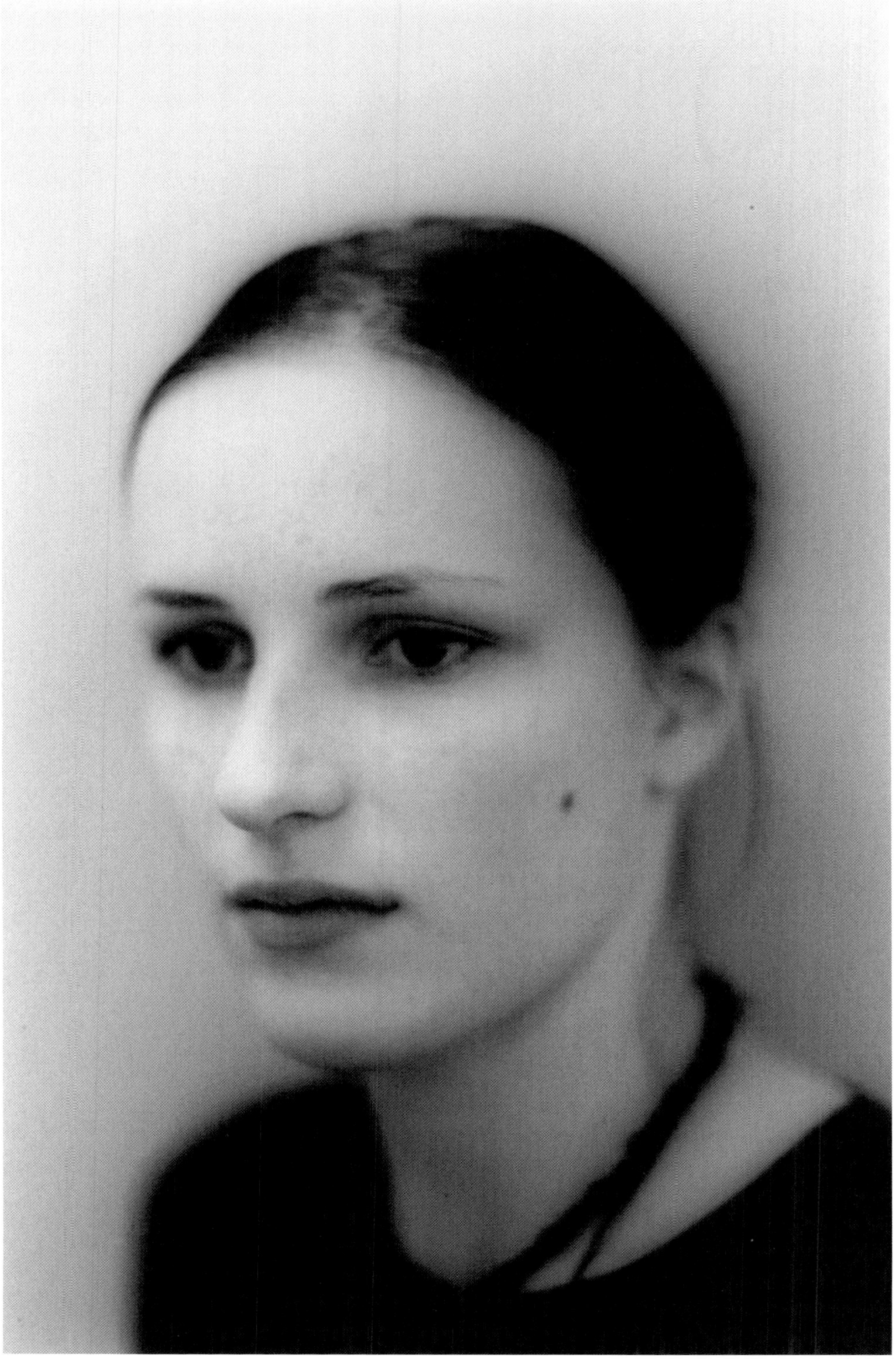

(PREVIOUS PAGE) 41 ARNO NOLLEN *Wakmae* 2002
42 ARNO NOLLEN *Wakmae* 2002

(OPPOSITE PAGE) 43 EDWARD STEICHEN *Will Rogers* 1923

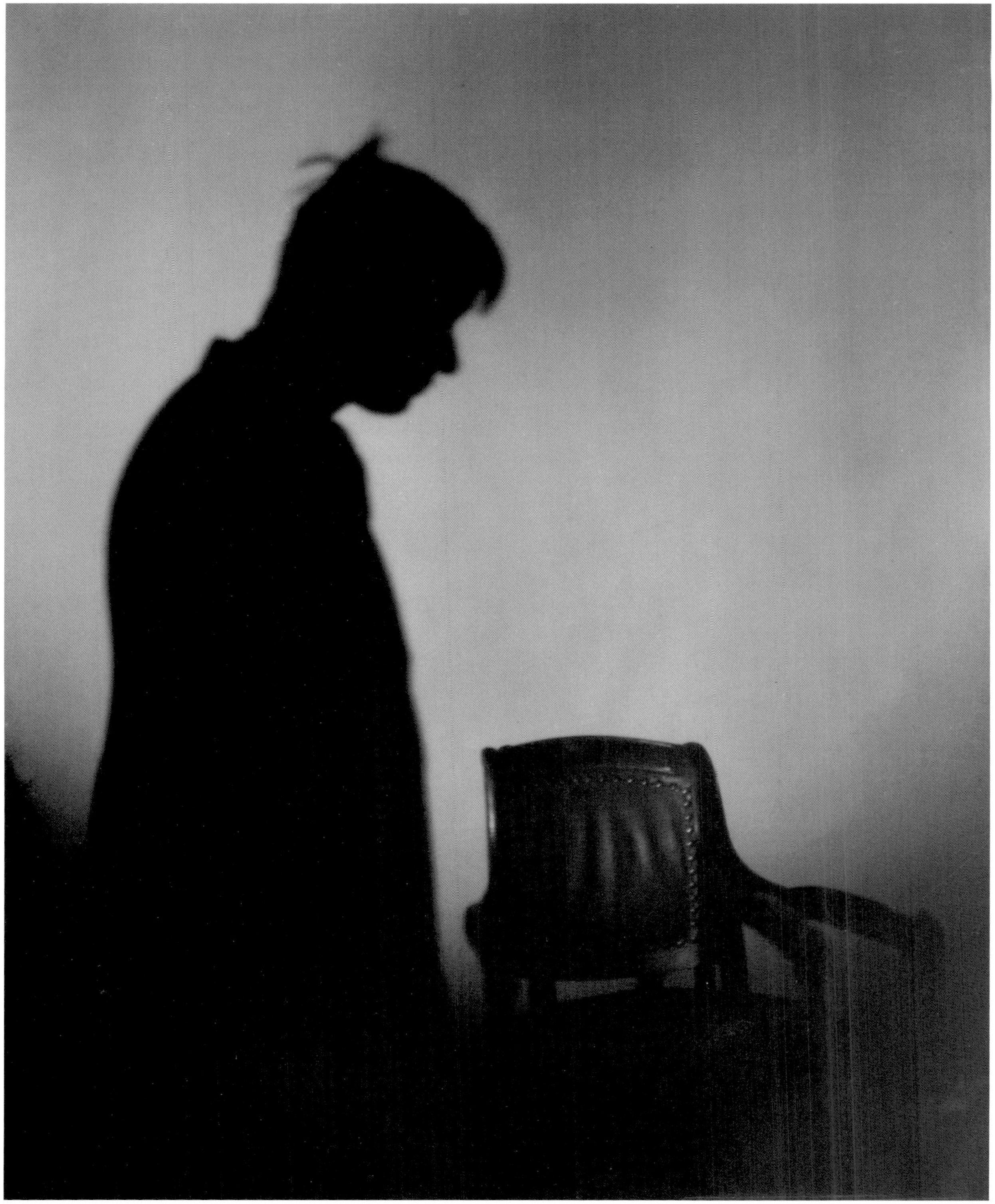

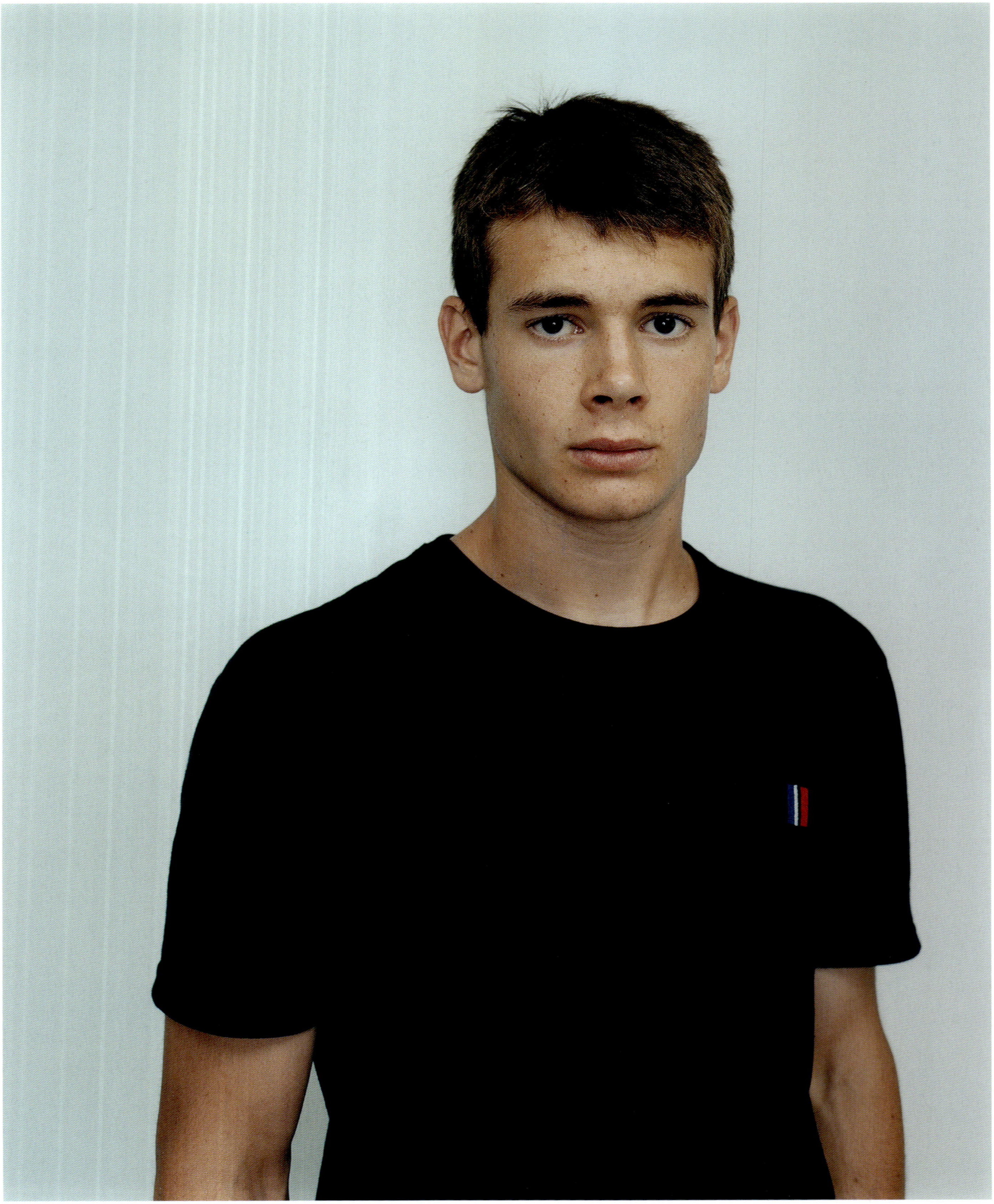

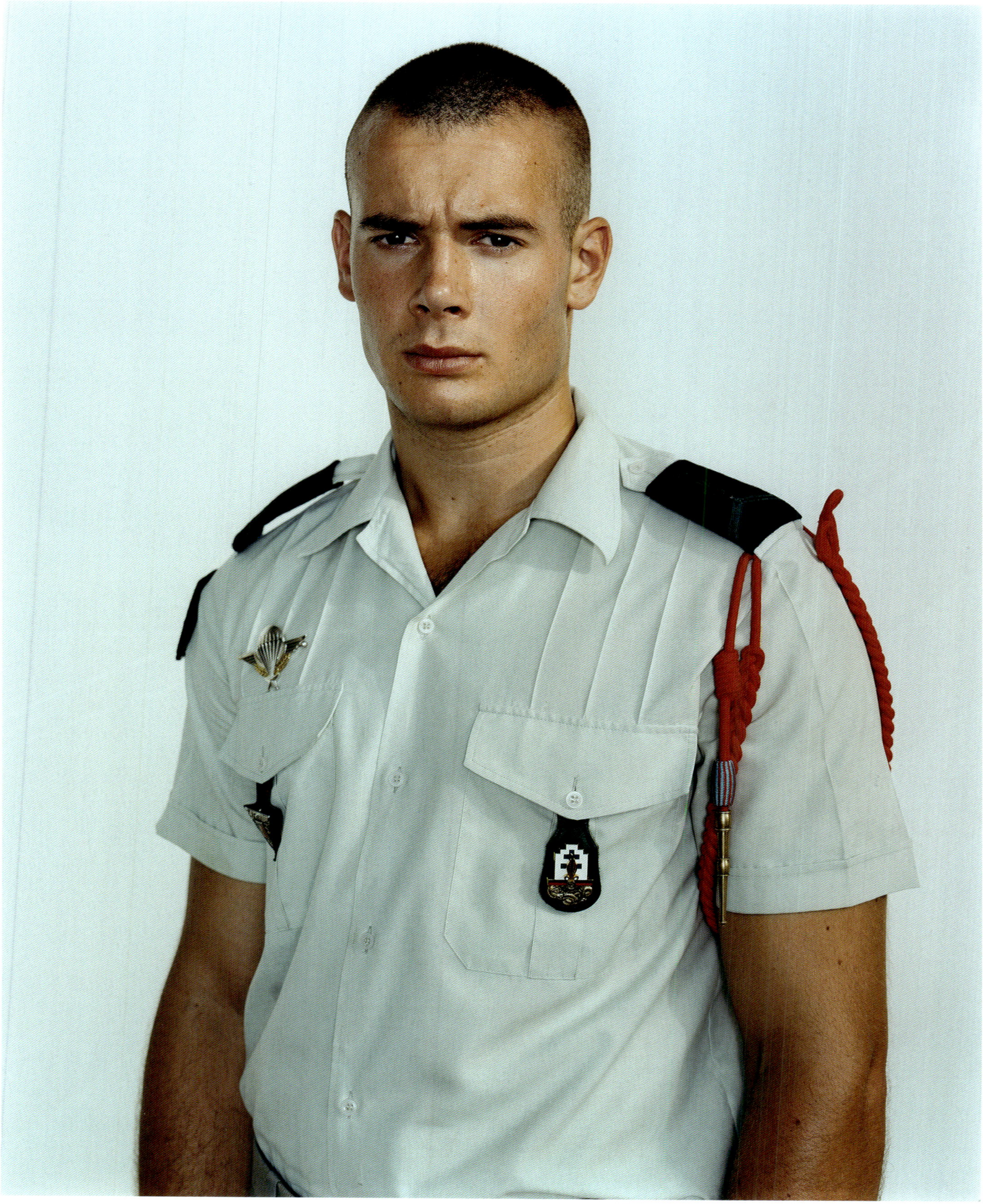

(PREVIOUS PAGE) 44 RINEKE DIJKSTRA *Olivier, Quartier Vienot, Marseille, France, July 21, 2000* 2000

45 RINEKE DIJKSTRA *Olivier, Quartier Monclar, Djibouti, July 13, 2003* 2003

(OPPOSITE PAGE) 46 EDWARD STEICHEN *Paul Robeson as "The Emperor Jones"* 1933

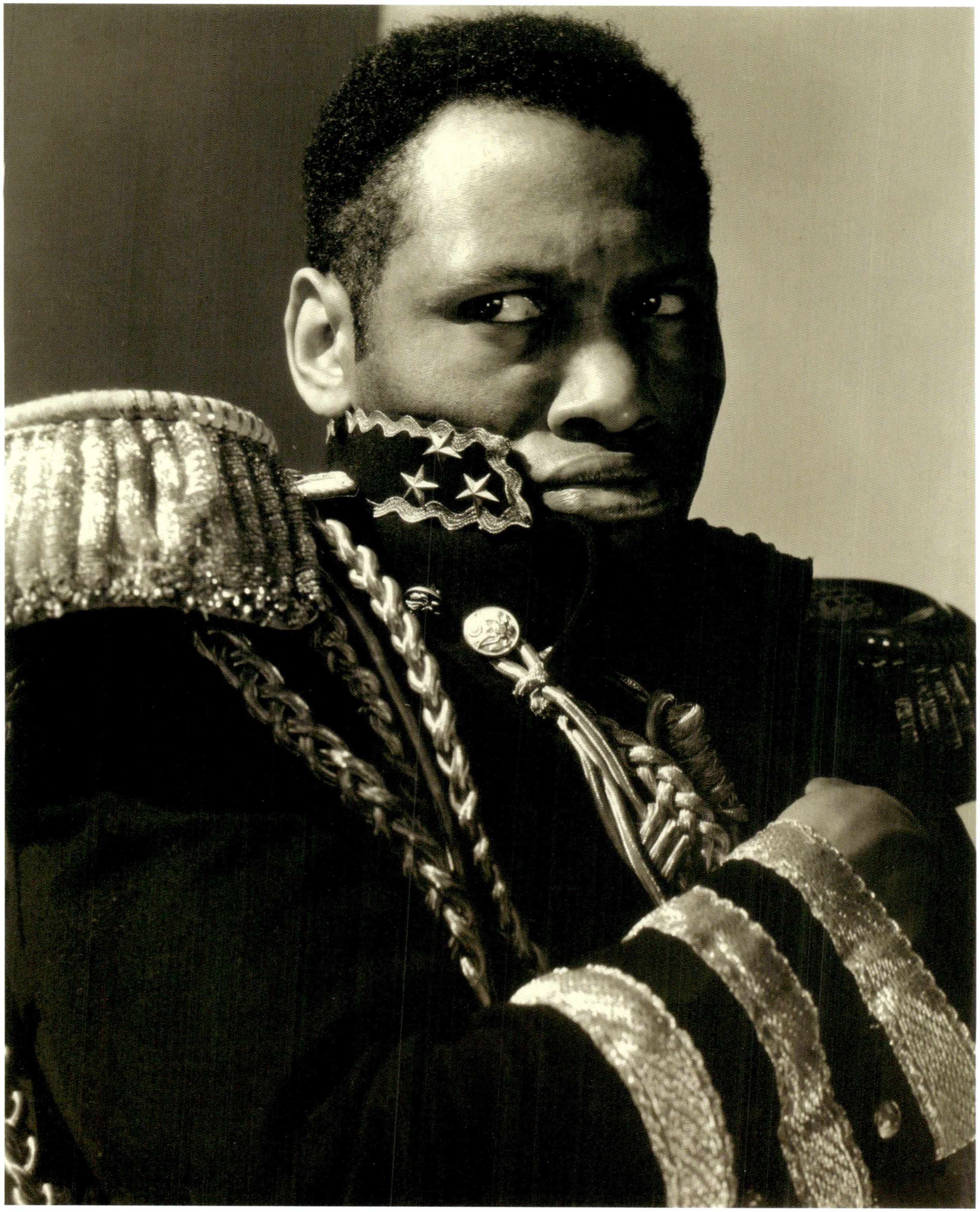

47 MAN RAY *Portrait of Nancy Cunard* 1925

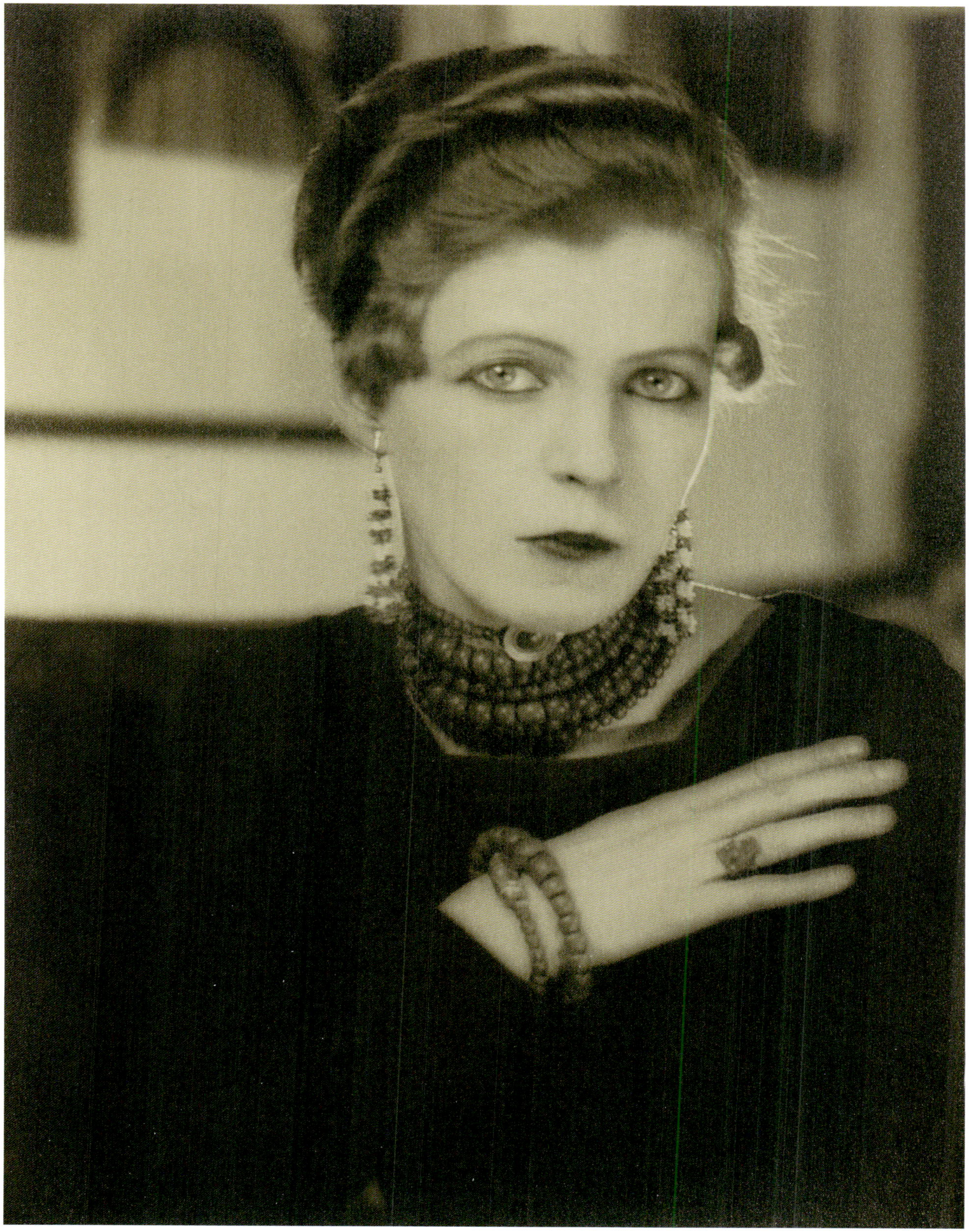

48 SEYDOU KEÏTA *Man with Flower* 1959

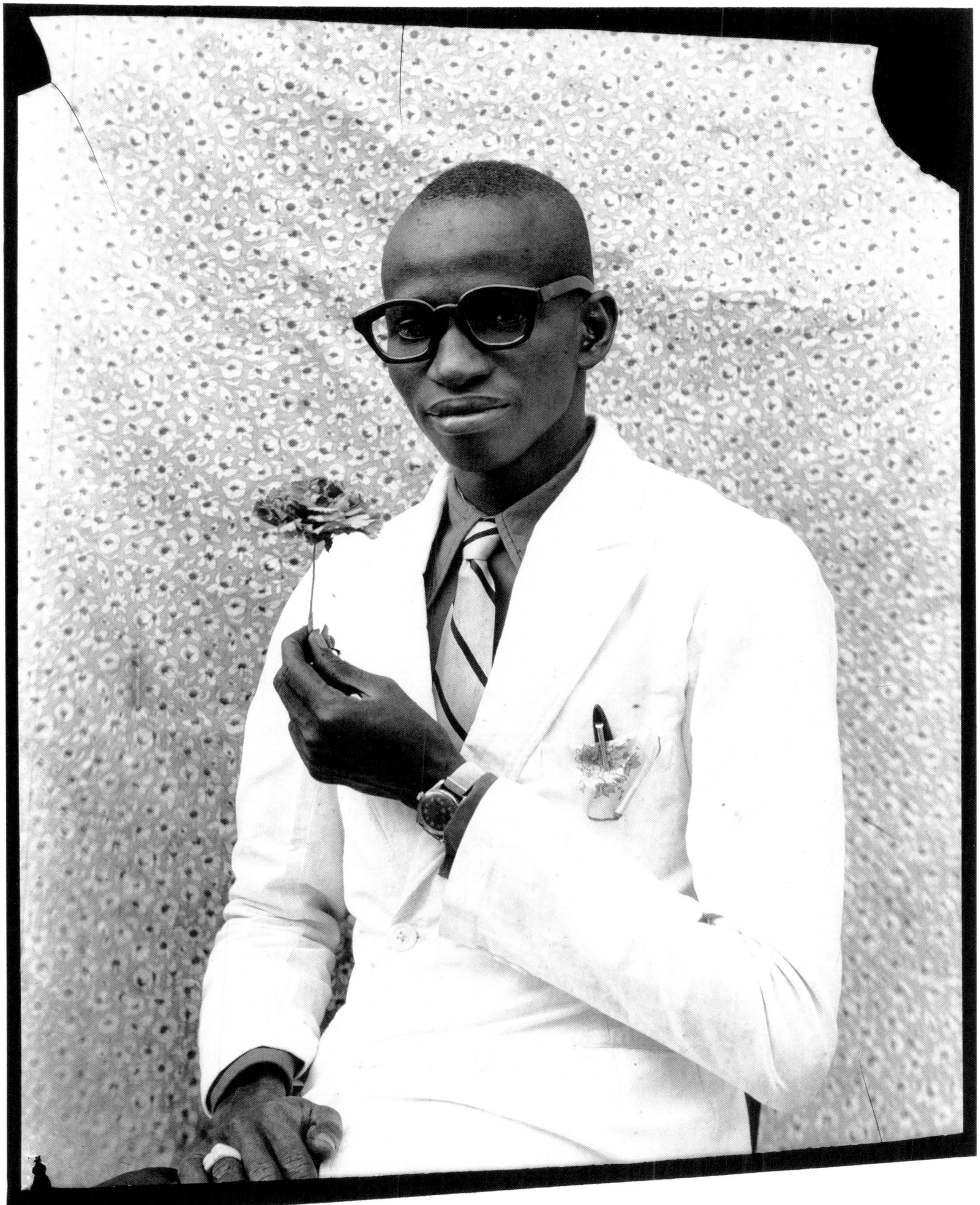

THE PHOTOGRAPHER'S CHOICE
CAROL EHLERS

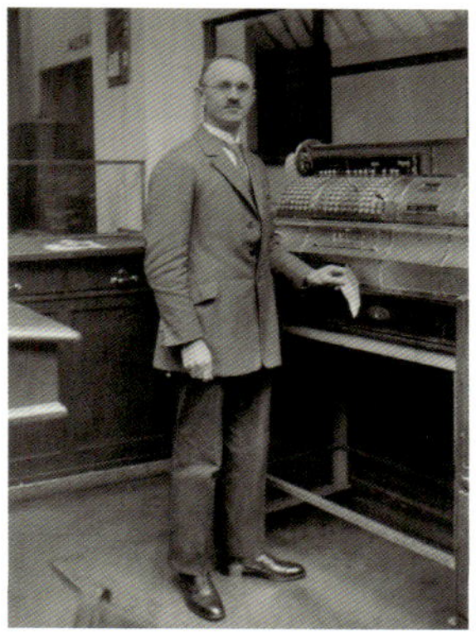

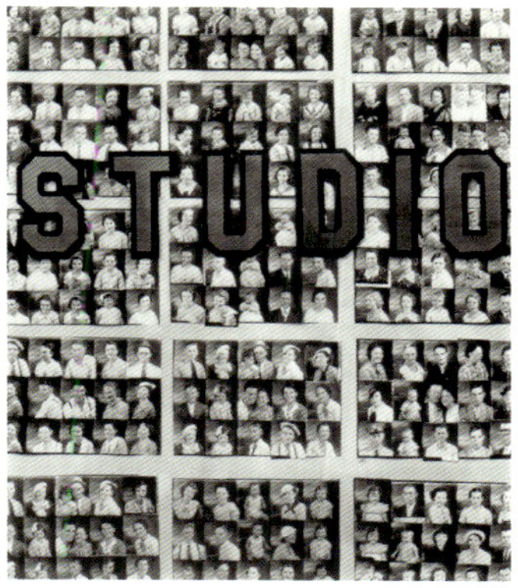

1, 2

Photography is the science and art of producing pictures by the action of light on chemically prepared papers. The discovery in 1565 that silver salts blackened when exposed to light occurred during the lifetime of Francis Bacon (1561–1626), the first modern philosopher of science. Bacon set forth in his *Advancement of Learning* the belief that in any field of knowledge the facts must be collected according to an accepted and prearranged plan and then passed through an automatic logical process from which correct judgments would inevitably emerge.[1] Because the phenomena of the world are infinite, in any field of knowledge the practitioner must somehow choose among them. A poet chooses words, a painter color and form, and a photographer chooses an image by framing a part of the world. The process of choosing phenomena is an act of judgment on the part of the practitioners and is based on their experience and knowledge of the world. No matter how straightforward a photograph appears, there is always a subjective interpretive dimension embedded in the image. When we view a photographic portrait, we are looking at an identity defined by the phenomena chosen by the artist. Thus we are seeing an image that is as much about the photographer and his or her point of view as it is about the person depicted.

This book opens with two images taken in the first half of the twentieth century: *Savings Bank Cashier, Cologne,* 1928 by August Sander and *Penny Picture Display, Savannah*, 1936 by Walker Evans. Both photographers were modernists who believed that truth lies in the physical details of the world. As a portrait photographer, August Sander sought to document an individual's body language, facial features, and occupational environment, in order to present the subject as part of a larger photographic project: a typology of twentieth-century man. The picture of a savings bank cashier (PLATE 1) is one of many that Sander took of workers and professionals in their occupational milieu. Sander's subjects appear to comply willingly with the photographer's vision of identity defined by occupation. Pausing in his work to assume a representative pose, the cashier looks straight at the camera. In 1929, Sander published sixty of his portraits in a book that he titled *Face of our Time*. Five years later, Germany's Government Bureau of Fine Arts ordered the book's printing plates destroyed and seized the remaining copies. After this disastrous interruption, Sander found it extremely difficult to continue his immense portrait project and he channeled his creative energies more intensely into photographing the landscape, a subject that had interested him since the beginning of his career. Around 1938, Sander photographed a group whom he identified as "Persecuted Jews." As in his other portraits, Sander documented the faces and body language of these individuals and then archived their portraits into his concept of a social whole.[2]

Walker Evans, like Sander, set out to document the social reality of his culture. He illustrated *Penny Picture Display, Savannah,* 1936 (PLATE 2) along with eighty-seven other

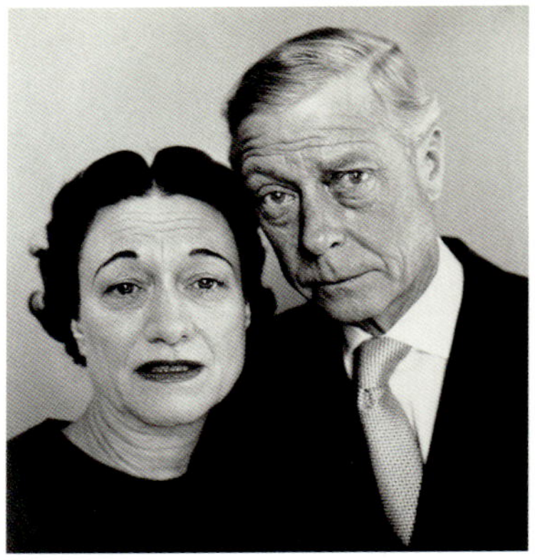

5

Depression Era pictures, in his 1938 book *Walker Evans: American Photographs*. By including his name in the title and placing it before the subject of his pictures, Evans emphasized the role of the artist as interpreter. This important observation is furthered by the opening image: the exterior of a photography studio on which two hands, painted under the word "Photos," point toward a dark stairway entrance. *Penny Picture Display* is the second picture in the book. The image, which includes the word "Studio," flatly identifies his subject: an accumulative portrait of the American people. The display comprises fifteen grids of fifteen individual portraits. They cover the entire picture surface and presumably go beyond the frame because the ones on the edges are cropped. The portraits, as the title tells us, are the everyday sort. We cannot see the minute individual pictures well enough to discern the character of the sitters. What we can see is the impact of them together – their display as a group. This is a picture about pictures and the cultural narrative that is embedded in our vernacular constructs. Whether he photographed the parlor of a Portuguese immigrant family in Massachusetts, a barber shop in Alabama, or, as in this case, the window display of a commercial portrait studio, Evans was creating a portrait of America.

Richard Avedon's portraits come out of a completely different time in America than those of Walker Evans. The great divide between these two important American photographers was World War II and the attendant deployment of two atomic bombs. While Evans used the camera to isolate cultural signifiers that reside on the detailed surface of life, Avedon actively sought to break through the worldly personas of his famous subjects in order to expose what he thought was their true character. Through his innovative use of a white backdrop or a bare studio wall, Avedon stripped away the supportive indicators of status conventionally found in celebrity portraiture, leaving his well-known subjects vulnerable and undeniably human. Avedon himself tells the story that just before taking *The Duke and Duchess of Windsor, 1957* (PLATE 5), he told the dog-loving couple that he had just witnessed the death of one of their favorite breeds – a pug. This story confirms that the artist had a direct, active role in the portrait. The anguish shown individually in the faces of his subjects is reflective not only of their personal horror but also of Avedon's existential world view.

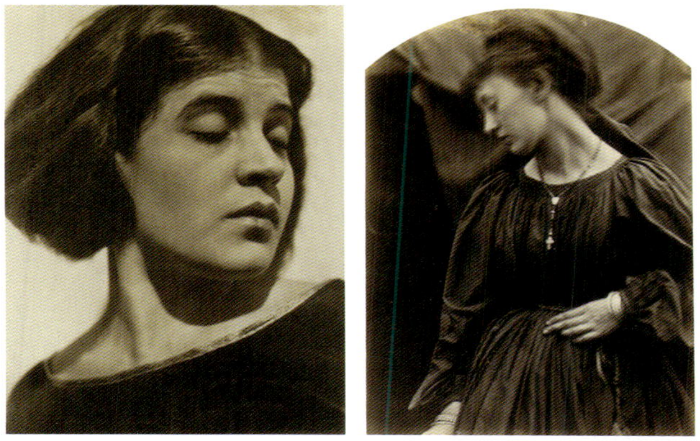

6, 8

Edward Weston's portrait *Tina Modotti, Mexico, 1924* (PLATE 6) is a powerful depiction of the artist's response to his lover and companion. In volume one of his daybooks, Weston writes about photographing Modotti: "Tina sat to me yesterday morning. We had long planned that I should do her as I have often seen her, quoting poetry – to attempt the registration of her remarkably mobile face in action. There was nothing forced in this attempt, she was soon in a mood which discounted me and my camera – or did she subconsciously feel my presence and respond to it?" Two days later, he writes: "my vision on the ground glass and my recognition of the critical moment for release were in absolute accord with her emotional crises…."[3] Weston's intentional use of a shallow depth-of-field softened the detailed clarity of this warm-toned platinum print. And his choice of paper and masterful printing technique emphasized the emotive deep shadows and sparkling highlights animating his subject. The artistry of the print is apparent to the viewer, who is made aware that Weston is showing us his vision of Modotti. It is an up-close and very personal view, so charged with the sensuality of encounter that the photograph takes our breath away.

Julia Margaret Cameron's portraits reflect not only her strong personal sensibilities but also those of her time. Born in Calcutta, Cameron was a colonial British subject who started photographing after moving to England with her husband and children. Her portrait of a woman with a cross (PLATE 8) was taken in October 1870. It is an image constructed by the artist to create a narrative. The woman in the picture (May Prinsep) is acting a part while costumed in classical garb and posed in front of a curtained set. Cameron has used the relatively new medium of photography to tell a story that was meaningful to her audience both historically and in light of their time. The story evoked appears to be about motherhood (as signaled by the model's hand lightly touching her belly or womb) and religion (indicated by the cross she is wearing). To a Victorian living in England, an image of motherhood was probably symbolic of both Christianity and of Victoria, their queen. In 1868, two years before the photograph was made, William Ewart Gladstone was elected Prime Minister of England primarily because of his program for dealing with the grievances of the Irish and their demand for Home Rule. Integral to his platform was a concession to the Irish Catholic Church that involved disestablishing and partially disendowing the Irish Protestant Church. Queen Victoria was the symbolic head of the Irish Protestant Church, and although she was not in favor of reducing its power, she recognized that the electorate had spoken and the bill had to be passed.[4] Cameron's biblically inspired image of a beautiful woman gracefully bowing her head while touching her belly may

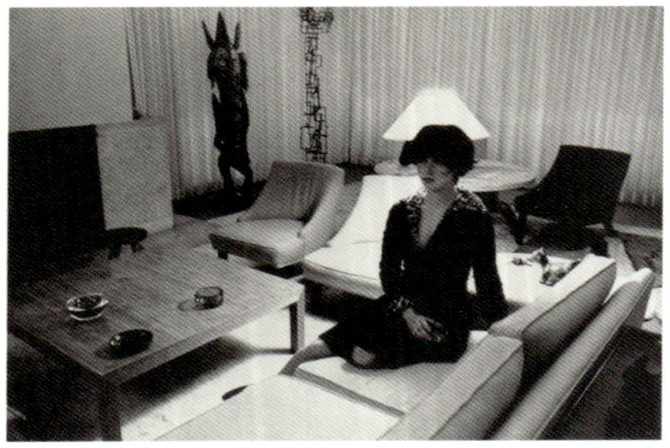

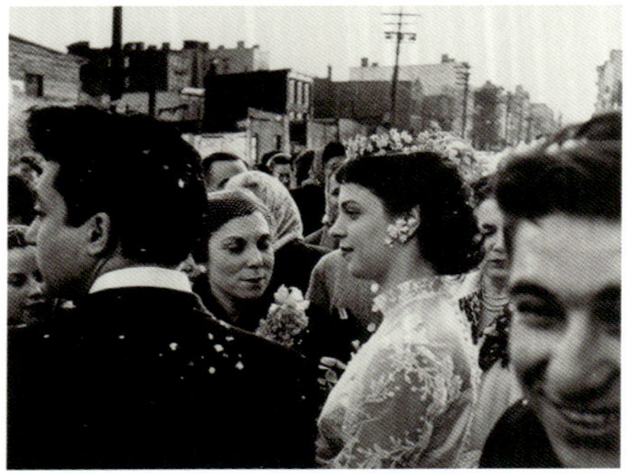

9, 10

have metaphorically illustrated for her Victorian audience the sacrifice their queen made for the good of the state.

The model in Cindy Sherman's *Untitled Film Still #50*, 1979 (PLATE 9) is the artist herself. She, too, is role-playing. All of Sherman's photographs from the *Film Still* series involve the artist costumed and acting a female part seen by the artist in re-runs of film noir movies from late 1940s and 1950s. Here she plays a sophisticate, dressed in a tailored black dress with leopard-fur trim, perched on a contemporary couch and holding a cocktail. Symbols of wealth and taste surround her: African art, abstract sculpture, and the long curtained wall of modern architecture. As with Cameron, Sherman has created a persona that is reflective of her society. In Sherman's case, she is addressing an audience who grew up under the influence of television and mass media. In Victorian England, Cameron used biblical imagery to illustrate contemporary ideals. As a postmodernist in America, Sherman appropriates roles from television and movies to examine the construct of female identity – a particular concern for her generation.

For William Klein, the world is a stage. In his photograph *The Bride*, 1955 (PLATE 10), the too-close face on the right beckons the viewer into the excitement of the scene with a twinkle in his eye and a grin. He is the stage manager/joker, drawing back the curtain and announcing that the performance has begun. Off his shoulder is a princess bride with a crown of flowers in her hair. She looks pleased, as does the matronly woman who faces her. The center of the picture is occupied by the space between them, from which the narrative unfolds in a swirl of white flowers: starting with the solidly placed

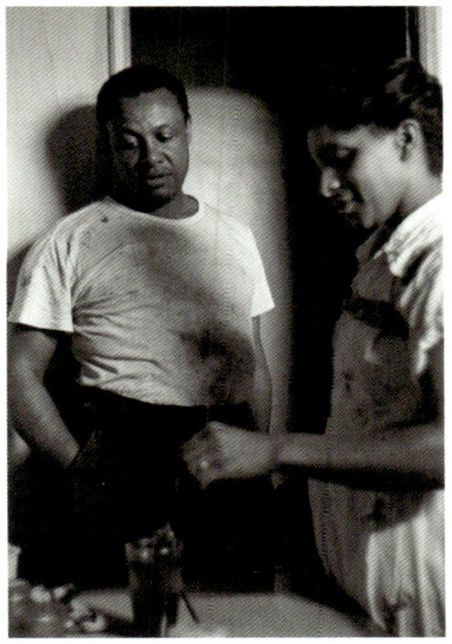

17

corsage on the matron's coat, up to the bride's crown on the right side, then down around the bride's ear across her neck and along her arm as lace. Petallike confetti drift across the groom's back and then disappear stage left following the path of the couple's gaze. An unidentified crowd surrounds the main characters – a chorus amplifying the action. Behind the crowd is the street, a backdrop of urban buildings. With the honed instincts of a great photographer, Klein framed his delirious everyman stories on the streets of "New York, Rome, Moscow, Tokyo, and Else-where."[5] They are raw graphic images infused with the improvisational energy of urban street life.

In his childhood and later as an artist, the streets of Harlem were home to Roy DeCarava. In 1952, DeCarava was awarded a fellowship from the John Simon Guggenheim Memorial Foundation to "photograph Harlem through the Negro people. Morning, noon, night, at work, going to work, coming home from work, at play, in the streets, talking, kidding, laughing, in the home, in the playgrounds, in the schools, bars, stores, libraries, beauty parlors, churches, etc.... I want to show the strength, the wisdom, the dignity of the Negro people."[6] *Sam and Shirley Talking,* 1952 (PLATE 17) is poetic testimony to DeCarava's insight into the lives of the people in his community. Through his broad range of velvety grays, DeCarava created a heartfelt image of the supportive companionship of marriage merely by picturing a husband and wife standing together in their kitchen. The husband leans against the wall, his face gently animated with thought. The wife stands in profile, smiling with her eyes lowered as she lifts a spoon from the glass before them. It is as though the artist quietly opened a door to his neighborhood, allowing us a deep breath of the warmth inside.

In the mid-1970s, photography began moving away from the democratic theater of the street into the realm of personal exposure. This cultural shift is exemplified by the 1973 televised documentation of the Loud family. "An American Family," a precursor of reality TV, followed the lives of Bill and Pat Loud of Santa Barbara, California, and their five children: Michele, Delilah, Grant, Kevin, and Lance. It brought to hundreds of thousands of living rooms across America scenes of the Louds' crumbling marriage and their son Lance's decision to declare openly that he was gay. A manifestation of the cultural change

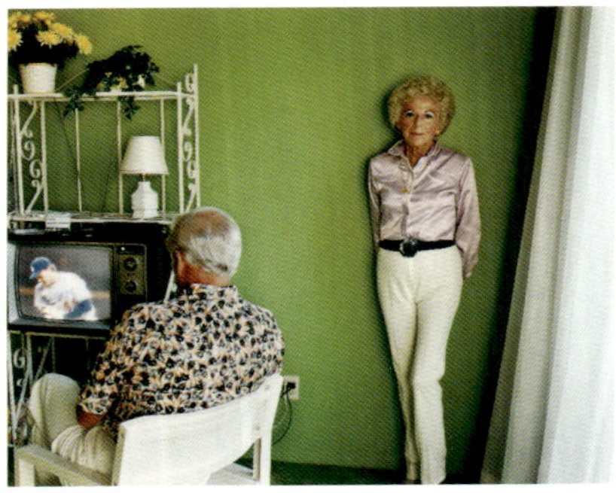

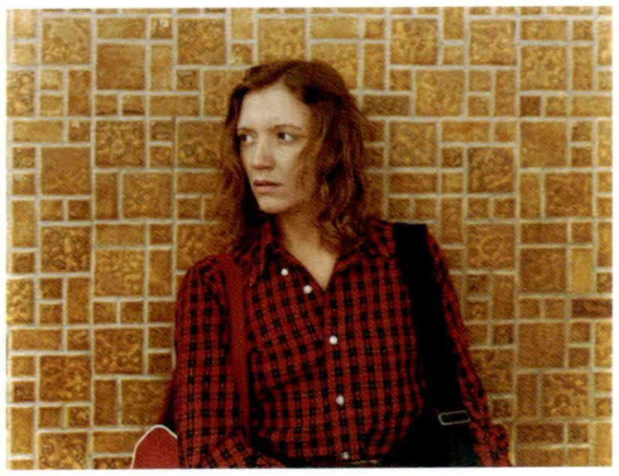

18, 29

in still images was The Museum of Modern Art's 1976 exhibition of William Eggleston's color photographs of everyday life. It marked a turning point in photography both in documenting the emotional nuances of the mundane and in the use of color as an acceptable element within art photography. This paved the way for images such as Larry Sultan's portrait *The Green Wall*, 1989 (PLATE 18) – one of the great photographs in the burgeoning genre of personal exposure. This color photograph carries a deep psychological weight that cannot be explained or dismissed. In a room of acid green, the artist's mother stands with her back to the wall. Plaintively, she looks straight at the viewer (her son with the camera), while her husband is seen from the back watching a baseball game on television. Sultan's riveting portrait of the isolating torpor in his parents' domestic life is so poignantly ordinary that we do not know whether to laugh or cry.

Stephen Shore's 1977 color portrait of the woman who later became his wife (PLATE 29) looks like a snapshot – the kind of picture an amateur would take on a trip. But in Shore's photograph, unlike a tourist's document, there is no historical monument nor is the person pictured holding still and smiling for the camera. Instead, the photograph's cultural reference is a prefabricated wall, and the woman looks away as though she is just about to bolt – a feeling enhanced by the red, white, and blue straps of her two shoulder bags. Her plaid shirt (typical student attire at the time) mimics the patterned environment she momentarily finds herself in. Shore's photograph is artistically transparent, allowing us to see the subject without being conscious of the filter of art. His vision is a distillation of the ordinary small moments and unnoticed places that comprise so much of daily life. Shore has given us an update on Walker Evans's portrait of America: in color, less formal, more transient, and prefabricated rather than handmade.

Stephen Shore's fresh portrayal of the detailed surface of contemporary America was influential to the generation of German photographers who were born after World War II and grew up in a reconstructed Germany. Among that generation is Thomas Struth, who since the 1980s has been photographing cities, families, and landscapes internationally. Unlike Shore's off-the-cuff glance, Struth's photographs are classically formal. By using the camera's innate Renaissance perspective, Struth pictorially organizes the phenomena of contemporary life.

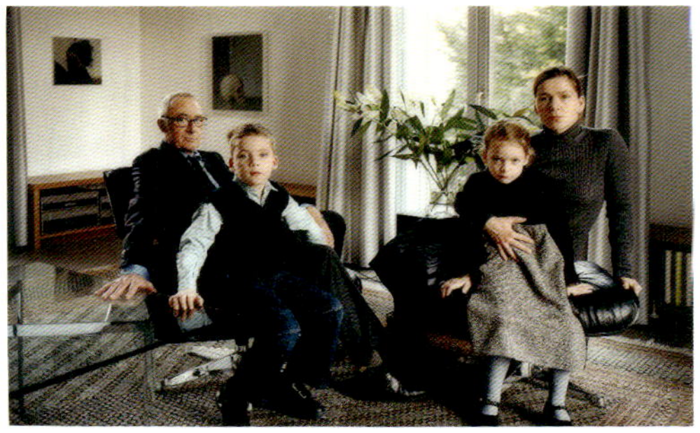

19

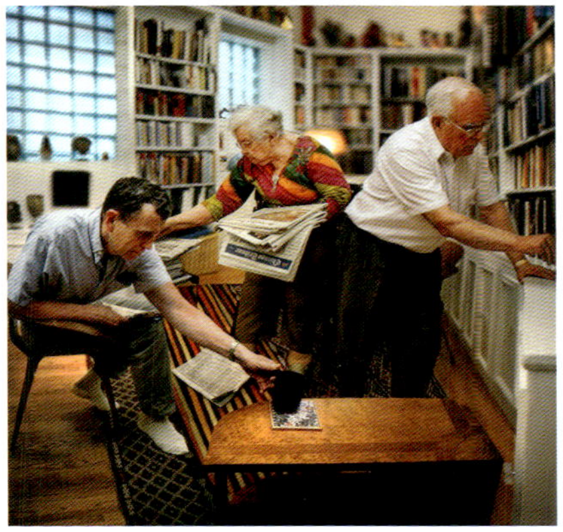

32

In *The Richter Family I, Cologne, 2002* (PLATE 19), Struth presented his former teacher and world-renowned painter Gerhard Richter at home with his wife, Sabine, and their two children. The large-scale color photograph is divided in half, with the parents leaning away from the center and from each other. This division feels less like a psychological rift than a balanced pairing of male and female. Behind the two males are a sound system and two paintings, one of a child, the other of a scull. Behind the females are a vase of white lilies and a glass door with a glimpse of light and a tree. The table on which both father and son place their hand was designed by the great German modern architect Mies van der Rohe. Similar to Struth's city pictures and landscapes, his portrayal of a family is a classically organized conglomerate of cultural and historical parts.

Ben Gest's portrait *Chuck, Alice and Dale,* 2003 (PLATE 32), taken in the first years of the twenty-first century, is not a "straight photograph." It is an amalgam of photographs taken by the artist, combined in his computer, and then output digitally as an inkjet print. As with Cindy Sherman, Gest synthesizes the phenomena of the world into a simulacrum of reality. But while Sherman's vision involves a postmodern deconstruction of the cultural myth of identity, Gest's is a synthetic cubistic approach to portraiture in the manner of his predecessor David Hockney. Gest has built an image of multiple perspectives that is aligned with his emotional knowledge of human relationships. The three people in Gest's picture are a family unit: two male partners, Chuck and Dale, and Chuck's mother, Alice. Their environment is shown as a home of collectors and readers. Though they appear to be in the same room at the same time, they were not necessarily together when their portraits were taken. Gest makes multiple photographs of different sections of his subjects' bodies and their surrounding environment, which he then compiles in his computer. The seated man reaching for a cup on a table is made up of many photographs (of his hand, wrist, arm, shoulder…) that are then combined to depict the gesture from several vantage points. There is in this synthetic family portrait, as in all of Gest's work, an isolated

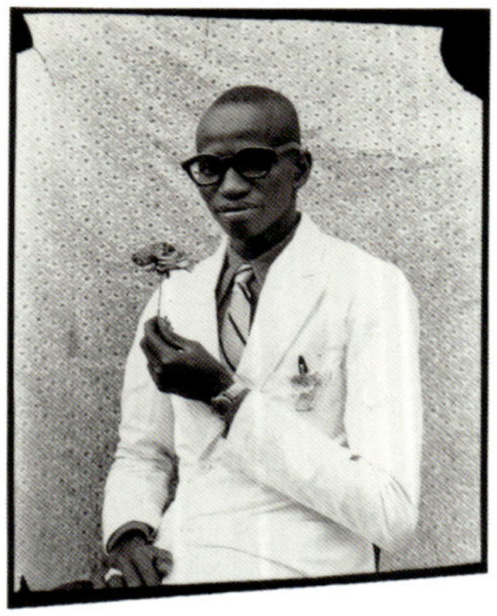

48

cohabitation of space. Seen pursuing their individual tasks, Chuck, Dale and Alice are together in the room – but literally not on the same plane.

This selection of portraits from the LaSalle Bank Photography Collection closes with a portrait taken in the studio of Seydou Keïta (PLATE 48). Keïta was born in Bamako, Mali. In 1935, his uncle, after returning from a trip to Senegal, gave the young Keïta his first camera. He started photographing his relatives and later took commissioned portraits with a larger format camera. In 1948, Keïta opened a portrait studio in Bamako. It was a great success partially because of his insider understanding of his subjects' desire to look their best. At his studio, a customer could choose from a myriad of props: clothing, hats, jewelry, radios, even a bicycle, scooter, or car. Costumed and arranged, they presented themselves for posterity. In this portrait, the sitter poses for the camera in a white suit and holding a paper flower. He has a pen carefully placed in his pocket, a watch on his left wrist, and a gold ring on his right hand. His open gaze is framed by stylish black glasses. Behind him is a backdrop of traditional patterned Mali fabric. In Keïta's portrait, we see not only the grace and natural charm of an individual but also a society in transition as it proudly takes its place in the modern world.

The invention of photography emerged from two branches of science: optics and the study of light. The camera obscura, an optical apparatus first described in 1038 by the Muslim scientist Alhazen,[7] was later diagramed in the Renaissance by Leonardo da Vinci. The Renaissance use of perspective radically changed Western thought: once a point of view was established, the phenomena of nature could be arranged into a field of discovery. By framing and thus separating elements from life's seemingly infinite offerings, a photographer presents his or her particular vision of the world. Though the process is often collaborative between the artist and the subject, the point of view is always that of the artist. In both art and science, discovery and knowledge are based on the practitioner's judgment of what is worthy of attention – in other words, on choices. The photographic portrait reveals not only the image of the subject but also the cultural, historical, and personal viewpoint that informed its creation.

CAROL EHLERS
Curator, LaSalle Bank Photography Collection

[1] *Encyclopedia Britannica* (Chicago, London, Toronto: Encyclopedia Britannia, Inc., 1957), vol. 20, p. 114.

[2] *August Sander: Citizens of the Twentieth Century/Portrait Photographs, 1892–1952,* ed. Gunther Sander (Cambridge, Massachusetts: The MIT Press, 1986), pp. 36–37.

[3] *The Daybooks of Edward Weston Volume I. Mexico*, ed. Nancy Newhall (New York: Aperture, 1961), p. 95.

[4] *Encyclopedia Britannica*, vol. 23, p. 128.

[5] *William Klein Photographs* (New York: Aperture, 1981), frontispiece.

[6] Peter Galassi, *Roy DeCarava: A Retrospective* (New York: The Museum of Modern Art, 1996), p. 19.

[7] *Encyclopedia Britannica*, vol. 4, pp. 658–59.

CATALOGUE OF PLATES

All dimensions refer to the size of the images.

1 August Sander
German, 1876–1964
Savings Bank Cashier, Cologne, 1928
Gelatin silver print, printed ca. 1928
9 1/8 x 6 5/8 inches

2 Walker Evans
American, 1903–1975
Penny Picture Display, Savannah, 1936
Gelatin silver print, printed ca. 1936
7 7/8 x 6 3/4 inches

3 Mike Disfarmer
American, 1884–1959
Untitled (Heber Springs, Arkansas), ca. 1940–45
Gelatin silver print, printed 1946
3 x 5 1/8 inches

4 Julie Moos
Canadian, born 1965
Mrs. Carr and Mrs. Thornton, 2000
From the series *Hat Ladies,* 2000–2001
Color coupler print, printed 2001
33 3/4 x 46 1/8 inches

5 Richard Avedon
American, 1923–2004
The Duke and Duchess of Windsor, 1957, 1957
Gelatin silver print, printed 1970
21 5/8 x 20 inches

Courtesy The Richard Avedon Foundation

6 Edward Weston
American, 1886–1958
Tina Modotti, Mexico, 1924, 1924
Platinum print, printed ca. 1924
9 1/4 x 7 1/8 inches

7 Richard Avedon
American, 1923–2004
Marilyn Monroe, Actress, 1957, 1957
Gelatin silver print, printed 1970
24 1/8 x 20 inches

Courtesy The Richard Avedon Foundation

8 Julia Margaret Cameron
British, 1815–1879
Untitled (May Prinsep), October 1870, 1870
Albumen silver print, printed ca. 1870
14 x 10 3/8 inches

9 Cindy Sherman
American, born 1954
Untitled Film Still #50, 1979
Gelatin silver print, printed 1989
8 1/4 x 11 7/8 inches
Courtesy the artist and Metro Pictures

10 William Klein
American, born 1928
The Bride, 1955
Gelatin silver print, printed ca. 1955
11 x 13 7/8 inches
© William Klein
Courtesy Howard Greenberg Gallery, New York

11 Gordon Parks
American, 1912–2006
Broke Price, former Hollis War Counselor, Harlem, 1948
Gelatin silver print, printed 1948
13 3/8 x 10 1/2 inches
© Gordon Parks

12 Eduard van der Elsken
Dutch, 1925–1990
Groenburgwal, Amsterdam, 1963
Gelatin silver print, printed ca. 1970s–80s
12 1/2 x 18 5/8 inches
© Ed van der Elsken / Nederlands fotomuseum
Courtesy Annet Gelink Gallery

13 Rineke Dijkstra
Dutch, born 1959
Vondelpark, June 10, 2005, 2005
Color coupler print, printed 2006
44 x 55 inches
Courtesy Marian Goodman Gallery, New York

14 Jitka Hanzlová
Czechoslovakian, born 1958
"Indian Woman," Chelsea, 1999
From the series *Female*, 1997–2000
Color coupler print, printed 2000
11 3/8 x 7 1/2 inches
Courtesy Gasser and Grunert Gallery, New York

15 Meridel Rubenstein
American, born 1948
Peggy Martinez, Santa Cruz, '64 Chevy Two-Tone, 1980
From the portfolio *The Lowriders, Portraits from New Mexico,* 1980
Color coupler print, printed 1980
6 3/4 x 9 1/2 inches
Courtesy Brian Gross Fine Art, San Francisco

16 David Hilliard
American, born 1964
Dad, 1998
Color coupler triptych, printed 2004
23 x 17 7/8 inches each
Courtesy the artist and Yancey Richardson Gallery, New York

17 Roy DeCarava
American, born 1919
Sam and Shirley Talking, 1952
Gelatin silver print, printed ca. 1952
13 1/4 x 9 inches
© Roy DeCarava 1996

18 Larry Sultan
American, born 1946
The Green Wall, 1989
From the series *Pictures from Home*, 1989
Color coupler print, printed 2004
17 7/8 x 21 7/8 inches
Courtesy Janet Borden, Inc., New York

19 Thomas Struth
German, born 1954
The Richter Family I, Cologne, 2002, 2002
Color coupler print, printed 2002
53 1/8 x 76 1/8 inches
© 2006 Thomas Struth
Courtesy Marian Goodman Gallery, New York

20 Tina Barney
American, born 1946
Father and Sons, 1996
Color coupler print, printed 2006
46 7/8 x 59 5/8 inches
Courtesy Janet Borden, Inc., New York

21 Carrie Mae Weems
American, born 1953
After Manet, 2001
Color coupler print, printed 2002
18 inches diameter
© Carrie Mae Weems

22 Nicholas Nixon
American, born 1947
Heather Brown McCann, Mimi Brown, Bebe Brown Nixon, Laurie Brown, Hartford, Conn., 1976, 1976
From the ongoing series *The Brown Sisters,* 1976–
Gelatin silver print, printed ca. 1983
8 x 10 inches
© Nicholas Nixon
Courtesy Yossi Milo Gallery, New York

23 Nicholas Nixon
American, born 1947
Heather Brown, Mimi Brown, Bebe Brown Nixon, Laurie Brown Tranchin, Brighton, Mass., 1983, 1983
From the ongoing series *The Brown Sisters,* 1976–
Gelatin silver print, printed ca. 1983
8 x 10 inches
© Nicholas Nixon
Courtesy Yossi Milo Gallery, New York

24 Diane Arbus
American, 1923–1971
Identical Twins, Roselle, N.J., 1967
Gelatin silver print, printed 1973
14 3/4 x 15 inches
© The Estate of Diane Arbus LLC

25 Mike Disfarmer
American, 1884–1959
Untitled (Willie Dettweiler, Vernon Higgs, Heber Springs, Arkansas), 1946
Gelatin silver print, printed 1946
4 1/2 x 2 7/8 inches

26 August Sander
German, 1872–1964
Boxers, 1929
Gelatin silver print, printed 1985
10 1/8 x 7 1/4 inches
© 2006 Die Photographische Sammlung/SK Stiftung Kultur - August Sander Archiv, Cologne/ARS, New York

27 Chan Chao
Burmese, born 1966
Mya Khaing, May 1997, 1997
Color coupler print printed 2002
35 1/4 x 29 1/8 inches
Courtesy the artist and Yancey Richardson Gallery, New York

28 Rip Hopkins
English, born 1972
Omirzo Salomov, 36 years old, Tajik: Engineer, Romish restaurant, 2001
Color coupler print, printed 2003
23 1/2 x 30 5/8 inches
© Rip Hopkins
Courtesy Agence VU, Paris

29 Stephen Shore
American, born 1947
Ginger Shore, Miami, Florida, November 12, 1977, 1977
Color coupler print, printed 1980
12 x 15 1/8 inches
Courtesy 303 Gallery

30 David Hockney
English, born 1935
Billy Wilder lighting his cigar, Dec. 1982, 1982
Color coupler collage, made before 1993
27 x 17 1/2 inches
© David Hockney

31 Dawoud Bey
American, born 1953
Toyia, Kelvin & Erica II, 1993
Eight dye dispersion prints, printed 1993
30 x 22 inches each
© 2006 Dawoud Bey

32 Ben Gest
American, born 1975
Chuck, Alice and Dale, 2003
Inkjet print, printed 2004
39 5/8 x 40 1/8 inches
© Ben Gest
Courtesy Daiter Contemporary, Chicago

33 Philip-Lorca diCorcia
American, born 1953
Mario, 1978
Color coupler print, printed 1990
15 7/8 x 23 inches
© Philip-Lorca diCorcia
Courtesy Pace/MacGill Gallery, New York

34 Edward Weston
American, 1886–1958
Johan Hagemeyer, 1925, 1925
Platinum print, printed ca. 1925
7 5/8 x 9 3/8 inches
© 1981 Center for Creative Photography, Arizona Board of Regents

35 Henri Cartier-Bresson
French, 1908–2004
Washington, D.C. (Robert Kennedy), 1961
Gelatin silver print, printed before 1974
13 7/8 x 9 3/8 inches
Courtesy the artist and Magnum Photos

36 Philippe Halsmann
American, born Latvia, 1906–1979
Richard M. Nixon, 1955
Gelatin silver print, printed ca. 1955–60
14 x 11 inches
© Halsmann Estate

37 Tina Barney
American, born 1946
Entrance Hall, 1996
Color coupler print, printed 2000
60 x 48 inches
Courtesy Janet Borden, Inc., New York

38 Manuel Alvarez Bravo
Mexican, 1902–2002
Frida Kahlo in Manuel Alvarez Bravo's Studio, 1930s
Gelatin silver print, printed before 1992
9 5/8 x 7 1/4 inches
Courtesy Throckmorton Fine Art, New York

39 Chuck Stewart
American, born 1927
Eric Dolphy, New York City, February 1964, 1964
Gelatin silver print, printed 2004
17 1/4 x 13 7/8 inches
Courtesy the artist

40 Dieter Appelt
German, born 1935
The Mark on the Mirror Breathing Makes, 1978
Gelatin silver print, printed before 2000
11 1/2 x 15 1/4 inches
© Dieter Appelt
Courtesy Kicken Gallery, Berlin

41 Arno Nollen
Dutch, born 1964
Wakmae, 2002
Gelatin silver print, printed 2002
15 x 9 5/8 inches
Courtesy Van Zoetendaal, Amsterdam

42 Arno Nollen
Dutch, born 1964
Wakmae, 2002
Gelatin silver print, printed 2002
15 x 9 5/8 inches
Courtesy Van Zoetendaal, Amsterdam

43 Edward Steichen
American, 1879–1973
Will Rogers, 1923
Gelatin silver print, printed ca. 1923
10 x 8 inches
Reprinted with permission of Joanna T. Steichen

44 Rineke Dijkstra
Dutch, born 1959
Olivier, Quartier Vienot, Marseille, France, July 21, 2000, 2000
Color coupler print, printed 2004
49 5/8 x 42 1/8 inches
Courtesy Marian Goodman Gallery, New York

45 Rineke Dijkstra
Dutch, born 1959
Olivier, Quartier Monclar, Djibouti, July 13, 2003, 2003
Color coupler print, printed 2004
49 5/8 x 42 1/8 inches
Courtesy Marian Goodman Gallery, New York

46 Edward Steichen
American, 1879–1973
Paul Robeson as "The Emperor Jones," 1933
Gelatin silver print, printed ca. 1933
9 5/8 x 7 1/2 inches
Reprinted with permission of Joanna T. Steichen

47 Man Ray
American, 1890–1976
Portrait of Nancy Cunard, 1925
Gelatin silver print, printed ca. 1925
11 x 8 3/8 inches
© 2006 Man Ray Trust / Artists Rights Society (ARS), NY / ADAGP, Paris

48 Seydou Keïta
Mali, 1921–2001
Man with Flower, 1959
Gelatin silver print, printed 1998
19 7/8–20 3/4 x 15 7/8 inches
© Estate Seydou Keïta
Courtesy J. M. Patras, Paris

ACKNOWLEDGMENTS

We are deeply grateful to Norman Bobins, Chairman, President & CEO of LaSalle Bank, for his stewardship in the arts, and to Thomas C. Heagy, Vice Chairman, for his constant and sound guidance of the LaSalle Bank Photography Collection.

Our sincere thanks go to Mark Nystuen, Executive Vice President of Marketing and Communications, for his cooperative spirit and unstinting support. We are also grateful to David Rudis, President of Personal Financial Services, for his understanding of the role of community in the interpretive process of looking at photographs.

We applaud all who joined us with their eyes, hands, and hearts to make this book. At LaSalle Bank, they include Deborah Peterson, Registrar, Nathan Keay, Curatorial Assistant, Anni Holm, Collections Photographer, and all the employees of the bank who watched the photographs reproduced in this book disappear from their offices and common areas for the duration of this project. At the Chicago design firm Studio Blue, we thank Cheryl Towler Weese, who provided warmth and enthusiasm while overseeing Tammy Baird's elegant design, Carolyn Heidrich's production management, and Amanda W. Freymann's supervision of the printing. Terry Ann R. Neff served as editor and contributed her years of knowledge regarding art and the book. Pat Goley led the team at Professional Graphics making the tritone and color separations, and Danny Frank at Meridian Press oversaw the fine printing of *One of a Kind: Portraits from the LaSalle Bank Photography Collection*.

Carol Ehlers, *Curator*
Whitney Bradshaw, *Assistant Curator*

Designed and produced by Studio Blue, Chicago
www.studioblue.us

Edited by t. a. neff associates, inc., Tucson, Arizona

Color separations by Professional Graphics, Rockford, Illinois

Printed by Meridian Printing, East Greenwich, Rhode Island

Available through
D. A. P. / Distributed Art Publishers
155 Sixth Avenue, 2nd Floor
New York, New York 10013
Tel: (212) 627 1999
Fax: (212) 627 9484

Library of Congress Control Number: 2006926436

ISBN 0-9702452-4-6

LaSalle Bank N. A.
135 South LaSalle Street
Chicago, Illinois 60603

Cover: Stephen Shore, *Ginger Shore, Miami, Florida, November 12, 1977*, 1977 (plate 29)